GRIFFITH'S OLD NUBIAN
LECTIONARY

PAPYROLOGICA CASTROCTAVIANA

Studia et textus   **8**

directa a José O'Callaghan

GERALD M. BROWNE

GRIFFITH'S OLD NUBIAN LECTIONARY

PAPYROLOGICA CASTROCTAVIANA
ROMA · BARCELONA
1982

TIPOGRAFIA DELLA PONTIFICIA UNIVERSITÀ GREGORIANA — ROMA

Contents

PREFACE

In preparing this revision of F. Ll. Griffith's edition of the Old Nubian Lectionary,[1] I have endeavored to eliminate the numerous faults in the original publication. In addition to frequent errors in transcription,[2] the text contains restorations that are often anomalous[3] or unsuited to the space available.[4] The reader is not always told how extensive a lacuna is,[5] or when the size is given, it may require adjustment.[6] At times Griffith did not accurately signal the presence of a lacuna: either he misplaced brackets[7] or omitted them altogether.[8] Further, he did not usually indicate how many lines of text he assumed were missing from the end of one page to the beginning of the next;[9] if such indications do appear, they are not necessarily accurate.[10] In addition, Griffith was not overly careful in reproducing the supraliteral

[1] F. Ll. Griffith, *The Nubian Texts of the Christian Period* (Abhandlungen der Königlich Preussischen Akademie der Wissenschaften Jg. 1913, Phil.-hist. Classe, Nr. 8; Berlin) 24-41. I have elsewhere discussed the deficiencies of the editio princeps in "Griffith's Old Nubian Lectionary," *Proceedings of the First Nilo-Saharan Linguistics Colloquium* (Leiden 1981) 145-150.
[2] 100.4, 12, 13, 14; 101.4, 7, 15, 16, 17; 102.1; 103.4, 9, 10; 105.1, 5, 12, 15, 16; 106.15; 107.6; 108.5, 10, 11, 14; 109.2, 8; 110.9; 111.9, 11, 15; 112.5, 14; 113.16; 115.1.
[3] 103.7; 104.1-2, 4, 10; 106.16; 107.10; 108.14; 110.1, 3-4, 12-13; 112.12; 114.2-3.
[4] 101.2, 9; 108.9, 15; 110.2, 4, 12; 114.2, 3.
[5] 105.16, 17; 113.16; 114.4 et passim; 115.2 et passim.
[6] 100.16; 101.8; 106.3; 107.16, 18-19; 110.13; 111.1; 113.15; 114.8; 115.7.
[7] 104.8; 105.8, 16, 17; 107.16; 110.4; 111.3; 114.6-7.
[8] 106.17, 18; 111.2; 113.15; 115.9.
[9] 100, 104, 109, 110, 111, 113, 114.
[10] 101, 105, 108, 112.

marks,[11] thereby obfuscating an orthographic system which is more clearly in evidence in the Lectionary than in any of the other Old Nubian texts now available.

In my commentary to the revision I note all the instances where I depart from the text of the editio princeps (except that I generally do not report readings differing only in the case of dotted letters[12]), and whenever necessary I show why the changes were made. All restorations which I introduce into the text I attempt to justify or at least to explain in the notes. I have sought to be more accurate than was Griffith in indicating supraliteration, in measuring lacunae, and in gauging the amount of text presumed missing between pages.

Since Griffith did not include a translation, our chief clue as to how he understood the Nubian lies in the interlinear Greek version which he added to his transcription. Not infrequently his version is misleading (e.g. 100.7 *ad* Mt 1:24) or simply incorrect (e.g. 115.7 *ad* Rom 8:3). After much hesitation I have decided to juxtapose to the Nubian text what *could* have been its Greek model, but I must urge extreme caution in making deductions from it. I follow the text of Nestle-Aland, *Novum Testamentum Graece*[26] and introduce variants only when the Nubian seems to warrant it. But the Nubian version is not always literal, and its interpretative tendencies make it unrealistic to assume that we can in every case reconstruct the underlying Greek (see e.g. 104.6-7 *ad* Rom 11:26 and 112.10-11 *ad* Gal 4:5).

I have added a tentative English translation, which, in conjunction with the commentary, should show how I interpret the text. Since our knowledge of Old Nubian is still rudimentary, much of my rendition is hypothetical. The occasional appearance of question marks in my version indicates extreme doubt; their absence should not encourage naive acceptance of the translation provided.

[11] 100.5, 9, 14; 101.1, 5, 11, 14; 102.8, 9; 104.4, 7, 10; 105.3, 4, 12; 106.1, 2, 8, 9, 10, 12, 20; 107.1, 2, 3, 14; 108.1, 6, 11; 109.1, 6, 7, 8, 9, 12; 110.6; 111.1, 4, 10; 112.6, 9, 10, 13; 113.2, 4, 10; 114.14; 115.6, 15.

[12] Griffith used the dot to indicate not only a doubtful letter but also one which, though damaged, is certain. In conformity with modern editorial practice, I dot a letter only when I have doubt about its reading.

When he compiled his index to the Lectionary, Griffith utilized a text anterior to what he published; hence a large number of discrepancies arise, as I have noted in my commentary. I have not found it necessary to provide a complete vocabulary of the text as revised but have contented myself with a list signalling the new words which the revision has yielded.

Throughout my work on this edition, I have enjoyed the support of the Research Board of the University of Illinois at Urbana-Champaign: I first studied the Lectionary by means of photographs obtained through a generous grant from the Board, and its members later supported my visit to Berlin, DDR, for autoptic examination of the manuscript itself. I am grateful to Dr. K. Schubarth, Direktor of the Deutsche Staatsbibliothek, who, together with his courteous staff, greatly facilitated my work in Berlin; and I should also thank Professors Hans-Martin Schenke and Fritz Hintze for making my stay in the DDR truly memorable. To Professor Schenke I am also grateful for his many beneficial paleographical comments, and I owe a special debt to Professor Hintze, for it was his "Beobachtungen zur altnubischen Grammatik" which initially inspired me to attempt to unravel the intricacies of Old Nubian. I should further express my appreciation to Professor J. Martin Plumley, who kindly made available to me pertinent texts from the unpublished material discovered at Qasr Ibrim.

Above all, it is my teacher, the late Professor Herbert C. Youtie, whom I must thank for the years he patiently spent in trying to instil in me the principles of critical method. My earlier work, first in Greek and Latin papyrology, then in Coptic studies, made me increasingly aware o the universal validity of these principles, and the effort now devoted to Old Nubian has but heightened this awareness. In appreciation for all that Professor Youtie has done for me, I humbly dedicate this edition to his honored memory.

6 October 1980
Urbana, Illinois

LIST OF ABBREVIATED TITLES

Abel = H. Abel, *Die Verbalformen des abhängigen Satzes* (*Subjunktiv und Infinitive*) *im Nubischen* (*Sitzungsberichte der Heidelberger Akademie der Wissenschaften*, Phil.-hist. Klasse 12.5; 1921).

Armbruster, *Lex.* = C. H. Armbruster, *Dongolese Nubian: A Lexicon* (Cambridge 1965).

BanG = F. Hintze, *Beobachtungen zur altnubischen Grammatik* I (Die "Partizipien"), II (Die Genitivpartikeln -n und -na), *Berliner Beiträge zur Ägyptologie und Sudanarchäologie: Wissenschaftliche Zeitschrift der Humboldt-Universität zu Berlin*, *Ges.-Sprachw. R.* 20 (1971) 3.287-293; III (Die sogenannten "Genera verbi"), *Altorientalische Forschungen* 2 (1975) 11-24; IV (Die Determination), *Nubia, Récentes recherches, Actes du Colloque Nubiologique International au Musée National de Varsovie, 19-22 juin 1972* (Warsaw 1975) 65-69; V (Das Futurum), *Altorientalische Forschungen* 5 (1977) 37-43.

Ben. = J. Barns, *A Text of the Benedicite in Greek and Old Nubian from Kasr el-Wizz*, in *Journal of Egyptian Archaeology* 60 (1974) 206-211.

Cramer = J. A. Cramer, *Catenae graecorum patrum in Novum Testamentum* 2: *Catenae in Evangelia S. Lucae et S. Joannis* (Oxford 1841).

Faras = F. Altheim and R. Stiehl, *Inschriften aus Faras*, in *Christentum am Roten Meer* 1 (Berlin/New York 1971) 487-508.

G(riffith) = F. Ll. Griffith, *The Nubian Texts of the Christian Period* (*Abhandlungen der Königlich Preussischen Akademie der Wissenschaften* Jg. 1913, Phil.-hist. Classe, Nr. 8; Berlin).

Horner = [G. W. Horner], *The Coptic Version of the New Testament in the Southern Dialect* (Oxford 1911-1924).

Horner[Boh] = [G. W. Horner], *The Coptic Version of the New Testament in the Northern Dialect* (Oxford 1898-1905).

Jakobielski, *Inscriptions* = St. Jakobielski, *Inscriptions from Faras and the Problems of the Chronology of Murals*, in *Études nubiennes, Colloque de Chantilly, 2-6 juillet 1975* (Cairo 1978) 141-151.

Massenbach = G. von Massenbach, *Nubische Texte im Dialekt der Kunūzi und der Dongolawi* (*Abhandlungen für die Kunde des Morgenlandes* 34.4; Wiesbaden 1962).

Metzger = B. M. Metzger, *The Christianization of Nubia and the Old Nubian Version of the New Testament*, in *Historical and Literary Studies: Pagan, Jewish, and*

14

Christian (Grand Rapids, Michigan, 1968) 111-122. (The numbers refer to Metzger's collation on 121.)

NA = E. Nestle, K. Aland *et alii, Novum Testamentum Graece,* 26th edition (Stuttgart 1979).

NA[app] = The apparatus in the preceding.

NI/74, NI/78 = The unpublished Old Nubian texts discovered by the Egypt Exploration Society at Qasr Ibrim in the excavations of 1974 and 1978 respectively.

NON = G. M. Browne, *Notes on Old Nubian,* in *Bulletin of the American Society of Papyrologists*: I-III in 16 (1979) 249-256; IV-V in 17 (1980) 37-43; VI-VII in 17 (1980) 129-141; VIII-X in 18 (1981) 55-67.

Plumley, *New Light* = J. M. Plumley, *New Light on the Kingdom of Dotawo,* in *Études nubiennes, Colloque de Chantilly, 2-6 juillet 1975* (Cairo 1978) 231-241.

Plumley, *Nubian Literary Text* = J. M. Plumley, *A Medieval Nubian Literary Text,* in *Sudan Texts Bulletin* 2 (1980) 34-41.

Schäfer-Schmidt, *Bruchstücke* = H. Schäfer and K. Schmidt, *Die ersten Bruchstücke christlicher Literatur in altnubischer Sprache (Sitzungsberichte der König lich Preussischen Akademie der Wissenschaften,* phil.-hist. Classe, 8. November 1906; Berlin) 774-785.

Schäfer-Schmidt, *Handschriften* = H. Schäfer and K. Schmidt, *Die altnubischen christlichen Handschriften der Königlichen Bibliothek zu Berlin (Sitzungsberichte der Königlich Preussischen Akademie der Wissenschaften,* phil.-hist. Classe, 20 . Juni 1907; Berlin) 602-613.

STB = Sudan Texts Bulletin.

Stricker = B. H. Stricker, *A Study in Medieval Nubian,* in *Bulletin of the School of Oriental Studies (University of London)* 10 (1940) 439-454.

Sunnarti = C. D. G. Müller, *Ergänzende Bemerkungen zu den deutschen Textfunden in Nubien,* in *Oriens Christianus* 62 (1978) 135-143. (The Nubian texts appear on 140-143; for the second see the revision of G. M. Browne, *A New Text in Old Nubian,* in *Zeitschrift für Papyrologie und Epigraphik* 37 [1980] 173-178.)

TR = Textus Receptus (Oxford 1873).

WN = F. Ll. Griffith, *Christian Documents from Nubia,* in *Proceedings of the British Academy* 14 (1928) 117-146. (The text in question appears on 118-128.)

ZPE = Zeitschrift für Papyrologie und Epigraphik.

Zyhlarz = E. Zyhlarz, *Grundzüge der nubischen Grammatik im christlichen Frühmittelalter (Altnubisch): Grammatik, Texte, Kommentar und Glossar (Abhandlungen für die Kunde des Morgenlandes* 18.1; Leipzig 1928).

Zyhlarz, *Sprachdenkmäler* = E. Zyhlarz, *Neue Sprachdenkmäler des Altnubischen,* in *Studies Presented to F. Ll. Griffith* (Oxford 1932) 187-195.

N.B. In citing the texts in Griffith and in referring to modern Nubian dialects, I use the abbreviations set forth in Griffith 86. References to paragraphs (e.g. §295) are to Zyhlarz. In the apparatus accompanying the Greek text, all sigla not explained above come from NA.

EDITORIAL PROCEDURES

I follow the principles observed in editing texts on papyrus, and the symbols have their conventional meaning:

[ ]   lacuna
< >   omission in original
{ }   superfluous letter or letters

Abbreviations are not resolved in the transcription. Dots inside brackets represent the number of letters presumed missing, dots outside brackets indicate illegible letters, and dots placed under letters mark them as uncertain.

In order to reproduce the text as accurately as feasible, I have introduced only word division. Printing requirements have necessitated simplification of the supraliteral marks: see below, p. 19. For Nubian δ I use $\mathbf{6}$.

In the commentary I have transliterated all citations from Old Nubian. For the enchoric letters I employ the following equivalences: $\check{g} = 6$, $\dot{n} = F$, $\tilde{n} = \phi$, $w = 9$. A circumflex marks long vowels (i.e. $\hat{e} = H$ and $\hat{o} = W$), and a horizontal bar reproduces the supraliteral mark.

DESCRIPTION OF THE MANUSCRIPT

Format

The Lectionary bears the inventory number Kgl. Bibl. MS. Or. Quart. 1019 and is lodged in the Deutsche Staatsbibliothek, Berlin (DDR). It consists of a quire of four double leaves or 16 pages. The pages run from 100 to 115, and the double leaves on which they are distributed measure as follows:

1 (100-1, 114-5): 21 (width) × 18 (height) cm.;
2 (102-3, 112-3): the leaf is broken into two parts, the first (102-3) being 13 × 16, the second (112-3) 12 × 9.8;
3 (104-5, 110-1): 24.1 × 20.5;
4 (106-7, 108-9): 23.7 × 18.2.

The outermost leaf of the quire (100-1, 114-5) is quite badly damaged, especially in the part holding the last two pages, and the lower half of the leaf with 102-3 is lost. Elsewhere the damage is less severe, though only two pages (106-7) preserve traces of the last line.

Whenever it is realistic, I have tried to calculate the number of lines missing from the end of the incomplete pages. Referring the reader to the commentary for details, I here present the results of this calculation, incorporated into a schematic representation of the arrangement of the quaternion (N.B. the numbers in parentheses refer to the number of lines presumed missing):

18

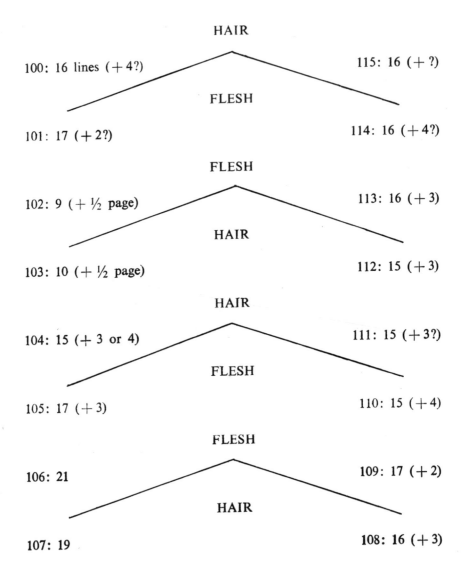

Orthography

"The writing," as Griffith reports, "is fairly even, without division
of words" (24). Rubrics head the individual lessons, and a colon
demarcates the components of the rubric (100.13; 105.1; 106.4; 112.3, 6).
In the summary of Mt 1:18-25 in 112.3-5 not only the rubric but also
the word *te* (line 4) is in red, and red ink fills the interior of the letter
phi in *iōsêphieion* in 100.6. To mark the end of phrases and sentences,
the scribe regularly employs two oblique strokes which generally slant
upward to the left. The first stroke is black, the second red, except
in 106.18, 107.11, 108.12, 112.8, 113.14 and 115.3, where the sequence
is reversed. In 103.4, 107.6 and 108.10 the red stroke is missing, and
in 109.12 both strokes are black. This "clause marker" appears at
times to be misplaced: 101.5 (it belongs after *gasknaula*, not before it),
107.1 (it belongs, not after *dinesô*, but after *eiriōōrô* in the next line),
109.6 (it would seem more suitable after *ālel* than before it). It is not
always present when we might expect it (e.g. after *kr̄ra* in 106.11),
and at times its use seems optional: see the note on 109.17. At the
end of a lesson or chapter, the scribe places a dicolon, the left half in
black, the right in red: 100.12; 106.3, 8; 112.2; and a dicolon also appears
in 112.5 (: : *choiākn̄* : :*k̄d* : : *par* : : —). Between lessons the scribe
may also add an ornamental series of lines and dots: 101.16 (see note);
106.3; 112.2, 5; 115.4. In 108.11, at the end of a clause, we find : : =,
in which the dots on the right and the lower horizontal are in red, and
the same pattern is very likely to be involved in 108.14, at the end of
a sentence and a line (here the surface is damaged: [: :] =).

The Old Nubian system of supraliteration is more carefully and
consistently followed in L. than in the other texts now available. I
discuss the features of this system — with particular reference to L. —
in NON VIII, to which I refer the reader for details. Because of printing exigencies I have replaced the various forms of supraliteral marks
with a horizontal bar, and when a stroke is centered over two letters I
have had it printed over the second. The complete set of photographs
at the end of the edition will enable the reader to see how the stroke
is made in each case.

If a word is divided between two lines, the break regularly occurs (1) between two vowels or diphthongs (e.g. *dou/ēsan* 111.5-6), (2) between a vowel or diphthong and a consonant followed by a vowel or diphthong (e.g. *ēne/ran-* 107.15-16), or (3) between two consonants, if the first is preceded, and the second is followed, by a vowel or diphthong (e.g. *pš/teu-* 109.12-13). For cases like *ē/gnouā* 101.3-4 and *eitr̄/snā* 112.7-8 see my remarks in NON VIII 56. In 114.11-12, *mašal]/oskl[ō* (modelled on *mašalosklō* 113.3) appears to be divided in accordance with its etymology (for which see Zyhlarz §51).

Date

In their first paper on Old Nubian, Schäfer and Schmidt noted in regards to the Lectionary: "Die Schrift zeigt grosse hässliche Buchstaben, deren Charakter etwa auf das 8. Jahrhundert n. Chr. schliessen lässt" (*Bruchstücke* 775). They also assigned the Stauros Text to the same period: "Die Schrift ist noch grösser und dicker als bei der ersten Handschrift, aber auch sie scheint dem 8. Jahrhundert anzugehören" (*Bruchstücke* 777). Later, in their second paper, they remarked that both L. and St. "höchst wahrscheinlich dem 10. oder 11. Jahrhundert angehören (nicht dem 8., wie ursprünglich angenommen wurde)" (*Handschriften* 606). What prompted Schäfer and Schmidt to change their opinion about the date is not evident. In the absence of securely dated texts in Old Nubian, it is risky to be dogmatic, but I suspect that the orthographic practices of the language may be of some use in dating the texts that we have. As I have argued in NON VIII 59, the system of supraliteration is analogous to what we find in Sahidic manuscripts of the ninth to eleventh centuries. If such manuscripts were the model for the Nubian scribes, then it seems likely that books like L., which show the system fully developed, are hardly earlier than the ninth century.

Content

As preserved, the manuscript contains a portion of a lectionary for Christmastide. "[It] extends from 24 to 30 Choiak [i.e. 20 to 26 December] and for each day there is prescribed a reading from the 'Apostle,' i.e. the letters of St. Paul, and from the Gospels. No guide is given to the place in the epistles from which the extract is taken, but for the Gospel the evangelist is named and the 'Ammonian' number of the first section is given [106.4, 112.3]" (Griffith 25); for the Ammonian numbers see Schäfer-Schmidt, *Handschriften* 603 and n. 1. The content of the text may be tabulated as follows (based, with modifications, on Griffith 25):

[24 Choiak   Epistle —]

             Gospel Mt 1:18-25 (cf. 28 Choiak)   100.1-12 (continuing from preceding page)

[25 Choiak] Epistle Phil 2:12-18   100.13-101.16

             Gospel Mt 5:13-20   101.17-103.10 (-?)

[26 Choiak] Epistle Rom 11:25-30 (continuing to 31: see 104.15n.)   104.1-15 (continuing from preceding page)

             [Gospel (?) —] (see 104.15n.)   104.19 (?): see 15n.

27 Choiak Epistle Heb 5:4-10   105.1-106.3

             Gospel Jn 16:33-17:26   106.4-110.18 (see 110.15n.)

28 Choiak Epistle Heb 9:1-5   110.19-112.2 (see 110.15n.)

             Gospel Mt 1:18-25 (cf. 24 Choiak)   112.3-5

29 Choiak Epistle Gal 4:4-7   112.6-17 (see 112.15n.)

             Gospel Mt 2:1-12   112.18-115.4 (see 112.15n.)

[30 Choiak] Epistle Rom 8:3-7 (or more)   115.5-16 (here the sheet breaks off)

             [Gospel —]   —

(Mt 1:22) . . . in order that there might be fulfilled what was said . . .: (23) "Behold, the virgin will become pregnant in the womb, and when she bears a son, they shall call his name Immanuel," a word which means "God will be with us." (24) And Joseph, when he awoke from sleep, doing as the angel of the Lord commanded him, took the virgin to himself. (25) And he did not know (?) her until, when she . . . bore her son as is proper, he called his name Jesus.

Choiak 25, Apostle (Phil 2:12): In this fashion, beloved, as you were obedient . . . always . . .

(Mt 1:22) . . . ἵνα πληρωθῇ τὸ ῥηθὲν ὑπὸ κυρίου διὰ τοῦ προφήτου λέγοντος · (23) ἰδοὺ ἡ παρθένος ἐν γαστρὶ ἕξει καὶ τέξεται υἱόν, καὶ καλέσουσιν τὸ ὄνομα αὐτοῦ Ἐμμανουήλ, ὅ ἐστιν μεθερμηνευόμενον μεθ' ἡμῶν ὁ θεός. (24) ἐγερθεὶς δὲ ὁ Ἰωσὴφ ἀπὸ τοῦ ὕπνου ἐποίησεν ὡς προσέταξεν αὐτῷ ὁ ἄγγελος κυρίου καὶ παρέλαβεν τὴν γυναῖκα αὐτοῦ, (25) καὶ οὐκ ἐγίνωσκεν αὐτὴν ἕως οὗ ἔτεκεν τὸν υἱὸν αὐτῆς (τὸν πρωτότοκον?), καὶ ἐκάλεσεν τὸ ὄνομα αὐτοῦ Ἰησοῦν.

(Phil 2:12) Ὥστε, ἀγαπητοί μου, καθὼς πάντοτε ὑπηκούσατε, μὴ ὡς ἐν τῇ παρουσίᾳ μου μόνον . . .

---

24 ἐγερθείς ΝΑ: aut διεγερθείς ΝΑ[app] (cf. Metzger 1)   παρέλαβεν τὴν γυναῖκα αὐτοῦ: "recepit ad se virginem" (interpres Nub. liberior; cf. Metzger 2)   25 τὸν υἱὸν αὐτῆς τὸν πρωτότοκον ΝΑ[app]: υἱόν ΝΑ (de τὸν πρωτότοκον vd. adn. ad 100. 10-11; cf. Metzger 3)

:p̄:

[π] εϲτακολ κιριϲ'[κον] νοϫλω \\ [ ]ε[ιϲϲῑ]   Mt 1:22,23

παρθενοϲιλλο τουλο 6ουντουϲαρρ[λ \\]

ϲακκον ογννιnνο \\ ταn ταϲῠκα

εμμαnνογῆλλ ⌈–⌉οκαρρανλῦ \\ θιϝρ[λ (?)]

5 θιϲῑ τιλλιλλω θλλλλ πελλ λογλλ[λ]

ϲαρραῦϲῑ \\ ϊω̄ϲηφιθιον ϲαλογ̣λ   24

λο πικκεn \\ ϲοαῆ αγγελοϲνῦ τακκ[λ]

μογρτλ τ[ρ̄θϲ]ῆ κελλικα αγῦ \\ παρθ[θ]

νοϲκα τα[γιλ θ]ναρ̣ιϲνᾱ⌈–⌉ \\ τακκοῆ   25

10 θι̣ῦριλγιρμε̣ν̣ναλω [\\] ταn ϲ[ακκα(?)]

τκ̄κῆn̲.[..ογ]νῆῆ \\ ταῃ [ταϲῠκα]

ϊπ̄ϲογ[ϲιῦ ο̄κε]n παγογκα ::

[χο]:[ῦκῆ :]⌈–⌉κε̣[:.] απος : εῆ τρ̈ϊτλο̄ οντ[λκρῦ]   Phil 2:12

[γο]γ̇εκε τ̣αγκα μω̄ω̄αnν[ο ± 6   ]

15 θϲογλγογρκ..ϲ̣n κε[λλω \\ ± 6   ]
     [ ]
  λ̣λ̣γφ[

– – – – – – – – – – – – –

(Probably four lines lost)

101

(Phil 2:14) Do all, without murmuring and insult (?), (15) in order that you, being without . . ., being innocent (?), may become . . .-less children, in the midst of a race hateful and evil, these in whom you shine, like luminaries in the world, (16) having the word of life, for my glory for the day of Christ, because I did not run in vain, and I did not toil without purpose. (17) But if I am to be sacrificed on the service-sacrifice of your faith, I rejoice, and with all of you I rejoice. (18) You also yourselves . . . come (?) with me . . .

Choiak 25, Matthew 31 (5:13) . . .

(Phil 2:14) πάντα ποιεῖτε χωρὶς γογγυσμῶν καὶ διαλογισμῶν, (15) ἵνα γένησθε ἄμεμπτοι καὶ ἀκέραιοι, τέκνα ⟨θεοῦ⟩ ἀμώμητα ἐν μέσῳ γενεᾶς σκολιᾶς καὶ διεστραμμένης, ἐν οἷς φαίνεσθε ὡς φωστῆρες ἐν κόσμῳ, (16) λόγον ζωῆς ἐπέχοντες, εἰς καύχημα ἐμοὶ εἰς ἡμέραν Χριστοῦ, ὅτι οὐκ εἰς κενὸν ἔδραμον οὐδὲ εἰς κενὸν ἐκοπίασα. (17) ἀλλὰ εἰ καὶ σπένδομαι ἐπὶ τῇ θυσίᾳ καὶ λειτουργίᾳ τῆς πίστεως ὑμῶν, χαίρω καὶ συγχαίρω πᾶσιν ὑμῖν · (18) τὸ δὲ αὐτὸ καὶ ὑμεῖς χαίρετε καὶ συγχαίρετέ μοι.

15 θεοῦ NA: om. Nub.   ἀμώμητα NA^{app}: aut ἄμωμα NA   ἐν μέσῳ TR: aut μέσον NA (cf. Metzger 12)

[ ]ⲡⲁ :

ⲟⲩⲁⲧ(?)]/ⲧⲟⲕ ⲁⲅⲉⲓⲃⲁⲛⲁⲥⲱ \\ ⲅⲟⲩⲣⲅⲓⲕⲕⲗⲁⲉ [ ]ⲁⲉⲕ(?)   Phil 2:14

    ⲕⲁⲛⲉⲗⲁⲉⲕⲉⲗ ⲙⲟⲣⲝ(?) [\\ .]ⲟⲟⲩⲕⲓⲫⲫⲁ   15

    ⲧⲟⲩⲁⲗⲗⲁ ⲧⲟⲩⲫⲉ ⲉⲁⲅⲟⲩⲕⲓⲫⲫⲁⲅⲟⲩ ⲉ̄

    ⲅⲛⲟⲩⲝ \\ ⲙⲉⲧⲉ ⲧ̄ⲥ̄ⲣⲝⲁⲉⲛⲟⲩ ⲙⲁⲗⲗⲁⲅ[ⲣ̄(?)]

5   ⲅⲗⲁⲉⲕⲉⲛⲛⲁ \\ ⲅⲁⲥⲕⲛⲁⲩⲗⲁ ⲉⲓⲛⲛ̄ⲅⲟⲩ

    ⲗⲁⲥⲓⲛ ⲡⲓⲗⲗⲁⲗⲗⲁⲥⲕⲉ \\ ⲕⲟⲥⲙⲟⲥⲁⲝ ⲡⲓ

    ⲅⲓⲧ ⲕⲟⲛⲉⲓⲗⲅⲟⲩⲛⲁⲛⲟⲛ \\ⲛ] ⲥⲁⲗ ⲁⲫⲉⲓⲛ   16

    ⲕⲟⲝⲗⲁ \\ ⲁⲛ ⲗⲁⲁⲕⲓⲅⲓ[ⲗ ⲭⲣⲓⲥ]ⲧⲟⲥⲓⲛ ⲟⲩ

    [ⲕⲟⲩⲣⲣⲁ]ⲅⲓⲗⲗⲉ [\\] ⲟ̄ⲛⲟⲛⲁ[ⲛ] ⲗⲓⲁⲉⲓⲙⲉⲛⲉ

10 [ⲥⲓⲗⲟⲉⲟⲩ]ⲛ \\ ⲧⲁⲧⲁⲛⲛ[ⲟ]ⲛ ⲕⲟⲣⲡⲁⲉⲓ
    [_]
    ⲙ̣ⲥ̣ⲥⲉⲗⲟ \\ ⲟⲩⲛ ⲡⲓⲥⲧⲉ̣[ⲩⲉⲧ̄ⲛ̄] ⲉⲁⲗⲗⲓ   17

    ⲁⲗ̣ⲏⲩⲥⲓⲁⲁⲱ ⲉⲩⲁⲣⲧⲁ̣[ⲕⲁⲣⲣ]ⲝ̄ⲗⲏ

    [ⲉⲛⲕⲱ \\] ⲡⲓⲥⲥⲓⲙⲙⲉ ⲟⲩⲣ ⲉⲓⲙⲙⲓⲁ

    [ⲅⲟⲩⲗⲁⲁⲗⲗⲟ]ⲛ ⲡⲓⲥⲥⲣⲉ̄ \\ ⲧⲉⲣⲟⲩ ⲟⲩⲕ   18

15 [ⲕⲉⲧⲁⲗ   ± 12   ⲁ̈ⲓⲁⲁ]ⲁ̣ ⲧⲁⲣⲁ

    [ⲛⲁⲥⲱ(?)   ]—

                       θ
    [ⲭⲟⲓⲝⲕⲛ̄ : ⲕ̄ⲉ̄ : ⲙⲁⲧ : ⲗ̄ⲉ̄ :   ± 6].   Mt 5:13

– – – – – – – – – – – –

(Probably two lines lost)

102

(Mt 5:13) ... As they are accustomed to give (?). It is no longer to become anything, except to be cast out and trodden upon by men. (14) You are the light of the world. It is not possible for a city standing on a mountain to be hidden. (15) And if one lights a fire (?), he should not [place *aut sim.*] it under a measure ... in order that it ...

(Mt 5:13) ... ἁλισθήσεται (?); εἰς οὐδὲν ἰσχύει ἔτι εἰ μὴ βληθὲν ἔξω καταπατεῖσθαι ὑπὸ τῶν ἀνθρώπων. (14) ὑμεῖς ἐστε τὸ φῶς τοῦ κόσμου. οὐ δύναται πόλις κρυβῆναι ἐπάνω ὄρους κειμένη · (15) οὐδὲ καίουσιν λύχνον καὶ τιθέασιν αὐτὸν ὑπὸ τὸν μόδιον ἀλλ᾽ ἐπὶ τὴν λυχνίαν ...

:ρ͞β:

ΤΙΚΚΕΝΝΑΝ \\ ϭ͞ΓΕΛ ΟΥ͞ΕΡΑϹΙ   Mt 5:13

ΜΕΝΚΕΡΑΛΟ \\ ὁΔϷΟϬϹΑ ϬΙΡΚΕΡΑ

ΕΙΓΟΥΛΟϬΟΥΝ ΟΥΚΚΟΥΤΤΑΚΚΕΝ

ΕΝΚⲰ \\ ΟΥΡΟΥ ΚΟϹΜΟϹΙΝ ΠΙΚΙΤ[Λ(?)]   14

5   ΚΕ \\ ϬΙΡΙΜΕΝΤΑΛΟ ΑΙΠΠΟΥ ΚΟΥΛ![Λ]

ΛⲰ ϹΟΝϬΙΛ ΗΥΓΙΡΤΑΚΚΑ \\ Ϲ͞ΤΗ͞ϲ[Ι(?)]   15

ΡΟϹΕ[Ν(?)].ΤΕΛΟΛΕ[...]ϲΙΟΝ ΜΑϷ[ΕΝ]

ΤΑΥⲰ[ΛΟ].[.]ΛΟ[....]ΜΕΝΚΕΡΑ

[ΛΟ \\   ± 10   ‑Κ]ΟΝΝⲰϲ̣[(Ϲ?)]

–   –   –   –   –   –   –   –   –   –

(Half a page lost)

(Mt 5:18) . . .until the passing away of heaven and of earth, neither an iota nor one of the dots which are on it will pass away from the law, until all are done. (19) Those—whoever these are—who undo a small one of these laws . . . , teaching men . . .

(Mt 5:18) . . . ἕως ἂν παρέλθῃ ὁ οὐρανὸς καὶ ἡ γῆ, ἰῶτα ἓν ἢ μία κεραία οὐ μὴ παρέλθῃ ἀπὸ τοῦ νόμου, ἕως ἂν πάντα γένηται. (19) ὃς ἐὰν λύσῃ μίαν τῶν ἐντολῶν τούτων τῶν ἐλαχίστων καὶ διδάξῃ τοὺς ἀνθρώπους, ἐλάχιστος κληθήσεται ἐν τῇ βασιλείᾳ τῶν οὐρανῶν . . .

19 διδάξῃ D: διδάξῃ οὕτως NA

[˙] p̄ᴦ :

ⲍⲁⲣⲙⲛⲁ̄ ⲟⲛ c̄ⲕ̄ⲧ̄ⲛⲁ ⲥⲟⲕⲉⲗⲗⲱ   Mt 5:18

ⲕⲓⲥⲕⲓⲗⲗⲱ ⲕⲥ̄ⲕⲗ̄ⲗⲱ ï ⲱⲧⲧⲁⲉⲛⲁⲉ

ⲡⲓⲥⲧⲟⲩ ⲧⲁⲗⲁⲱ ⲁⲗⲗⲁ ⲟⲩⲉⲗⲉⲛⲁⲉ

ⲧⲉⲃ̄ⲁⲓⲗⲁ ⲥⲟⲕⲁⲗⲉⲛⲁ \ ⲉⲓⲙⲙⲁ̄ⲅⲟ[ⲩ]

5   ⲛⲁ ⲗⲩⲧⲁⲕⲉⲣⲁⲛ ⲡⲁⲩⲟⲩⲕⲁ \\ ⲉⲛ̄ ⲥ̄   19

[ⲥ]ⲁⲛⲁ ⲉⲛ̄ ⲧⲉⲁⲅⲟⲩⲗⲁ ⲙⲉⲕⲕⲓⲁ ⲟⲩ

ⲉⲕⲕⲁ ⲕⲟⲩⲥ[ⲗ̄ⲅⲟⲩ]ⲗ ⲉⲓⲅⲟⲩⲕⲁ̣ [ⲟ]ⲩⲗ

[ⲗⲓ]ⲃⲁ ⲧⲟⲩⲕ.[. . . .].ⲉ[. .].[. .].ⲱ

[. . . .].[. .].[

10   [± 25   ]ⲩ

– – – – – – – – – – –

(Half a page lost)

(Rom 11:25)... because... has happened to Israel, until the fulness of the nations comes in. (26) Thus all Israel is saved, as it was written: "He comes from Sion, the one who saves, to turn away godlessness from Jacob. (27) And this is my covenant... when I take away their sins." (28) According to the Gospel they are enemies through you, but according to the election they are beloved through the fathers. (29) The gifts of God... (30)... you (?)...

(Rom 11:25)... ὅτι πώρωσις ἀπὸ μέρους τῷ Ἰσραὴλ γέγονεν ἄχρι οὗ τὸ πλήρωμα τῶν ἐθνῶν εἰσέλθῃ (26) καὶ οὕτως πᾶς Ἰσραὴλ σωθήσεται, καθὼς γέγραπται · ἥξει ἐκ Σιὼν ὁ ῥυόμενος, ἀποστρέψει ἀσεβείας ἀπὸ Ἰακώβ. (27) καὶ αὕτη αὐτοῖς ἡ παρ' ἐμοῦ διαθήκη, ὅταν ἀφέλωμαι τὰς ἁμαρτίας αὐτῶν. (28) κατὰ μὲν τὸ εὐαγγέλιον ἐχθροὶ δι' ὑμᾶς, κατὰ δὲ τὴν ἐκλογὴν ἀγαπητοὶ διὰ τοὺς πατέρας · (29) ἀμεταμέλητα γὰρ τὰ χαρίσματα καὶ ἡ κλῆσις τοῦ θεοῦ. (30) ὥσπερ γὰρ ὑμεῖς...

26 ἀποστρέψει NA: aut καὶ ἀποστρέψει TR (G. ad loc.: "Or for καὶ ἀποστρέψει read ἀπόστρεψαι " [sic pro ἀποστρέψαι]; sed interpres Nub. liberior)

: $\overline{\text{ΡΛ}}$ [᾿]

[.]ⲉⲗⲗⲱ ⲓ̈ⲥⲣⲁⲏⲗⲓ ⲅ ⲓⲗⲗⲉ ⲇ ⲟⲩⲗⲗⲁ ⲥ[ⲁ]   Rom 11:25

[ⲣ]ⲁ ⲥⲓ ⲛ \\ ⲥⲓⲡⲡⲓ ⲅ ⲟⲩⲛ ⲕ ⲓⲣⲓ ⲥⲓⲧ ⲛ⳽

[ⲧ]ⲟⲣⲁ ⲕ ⲓⲣⲉⲗⲗⲱ ⲕ̄ⲥⲕⲓⲗⲗⲱ \\ ⲉⲓⲕⲁⲣ[ⲓ]   26

[ⲅ]ⲣ⳽ⲗⲟ ⲓ̈ⲥⲣⲁⲏⲗⲓ ⲟⲩⲁⲧⲧⲟ ⲥⲁⲣⲧⲁ

5   ⲕ ⲟⲛⲁ \\ ⲡⲁⲣⲧⲁ ⲕⲉ ⲥⲓ ⲛ ⲕⲉⲗⲗⲱ \\ ⲕ[ⲏ̄]

ⲙⲁ ⲥ ⲓⲱ̄ⲛ ⲓ⳽ⲕⲉⲧⲁⲗ ⲁ ⲩⲗⲉⲗ \\ ⲅ ⲏ̄[ⲣ]

ⲧⲉⲛ ⲓ ⲁ [_] [_] ⲧⲁⲗⲗ ⲓ ⲕⲓ ⲫ ⲕⲁ ⲛⲉ ⲕⲁ ⲓ̈⳽ⲕ ⲱ

[ⲃ ⲓⲟ̄ \\ ⲟⲛ] ⲕ ⲉⲧⲁⲗ ⲉⲓ ⲛ ⲛⲟ ⲁ ⲛ ⲁ ⲓ ⲅ ⲓⲣ   27

ⲧ̣ [(ⲓ)ⲗ 3-4] ⲁⲗⲉⲛ \\ ⲧⲉⲛ ⲥ ⲁ ⲡⲉⲅ ⲟⲩ[ⲕ]

10 ⲟ̣ⲥ̣[ⲓ]ⲣ̣ⲁ̣[6]ⲉ ⲉⲣ ⲓ ⲧⲁ ⲩ ⲕⲁⲱ̄⳽ \\ ⲉⲁ ⲩⲉⲛ [ⲕⲉ]   28

ⲅⲁ ⲅ ⲣ⳽ⲗⲉ ⲟⲩ ⲕ ⲕⲁ ⲉ̄ⲅ ⲟⲩ ⲉ̄ ⲗⲱ ⲟⲩⲣ ⲓⲟ̄ⲉ [ⲱ⳽]

ⲥ ⲁ ⲥ ⲧ ⲛ̄ ⲕⲉ ⲅ ⲁ ⲅ ⲣ̣[⳽]ⲉⲓ ⲟⲛ ⲟ ⲛⲧⲁ ⲕ ⲣ̣[⳽]

ⲅ ⲟⲩ ⲉ̄ ⲗ ⲱ ⲡ ⲁ ⲡⲓ̣[ⲅ ⲟⲩ ⲗ ⲟ ⲉ]ⲱ̄⳽ \\ ⲧ̣[⳽ⲗ ⲛ̄]   29

ⲧ ̣ ⲧ ⲧ ̣ [ⲅ ⲟⲩ ⲗ ⲗ ⲉ   X   - ⲁ ⲉ ⲕ ⲉ ⲗ   X   ]

15 ⲟⲩ ⲣ̣ [30

— — — — — — — — — —

(Three or four lines lost)

Choiak 27, Apostle (Heb 5:4): And no one is to take honor on himself, except the one called by God, like Aaron. (5) Thus it was not for Christ to become high priest and take honor on himself, but the one who said to him: "You are my son," and "as for you, I have begotten you today," (6) as he says in a(nother) passage (?): "You are priest forever in accordance with the order of Melchizedek"; (7) who, in the days of his flesh ... and prayers to one able to save him from death, with supplication and ..., from ... (8) ... the one who is the Son ... obedience (?) ...

(Heb 5:4) καὶ οὐχ ἑαυτῷ τις λαμβάνει τὴν τιμὴν ἀλλὰ ὁ καλούμενος ὑπὸ τοῦ θεοῦ καθώσπερ καὶ Ἀαρών. (5) οὕτως καὶ ὁ Χριστὸς οὐχ ἑαυτὸν ἐδόξασεν γενηθῆναι ἀρχιερέα ἀλλ᾽ ὁ λαλήσας πρὸς αὐτόν · υἱός μου εἶ, σὺ ἐγὼ σήμερον γεγέννηκά σε · (6) καθὼς καὶ ἐν ἑτέρῳ λέγει · σὺ ἱερεὺς εἰς τὸν αἰῶνα κατὰ τὴν τάξιν Μελχισέδεκ, (7) ὃς ἐν ταῖς ἡμέραις τῆς σαρκὸς αὐτοῦ δεήσεις τε καὶ ἱκετηρίας πρὸς τὸν δυνάμενον σῴζειν αὐτὸν ἐκ θανάτου μετὰ κραυγῆς ἰσχυρᾶς καὶ δακρύων προσενέγκας καὶ εἰσακουσθεὶς ἀπὸ τῆς εὐλαβείας, (8) καίπερ ὢν υἱός, ἔμαθεν ἀφ᾽ ὧν ἔπαθεν τὴν ὑπακοήν,

4 ὁ καλούμενος TR: καλούμενος NA   5 εἶ, σὺ: vd. adn. ad 105.6-7

:р̄є:

ΧΟΙⲆΚΝ̄ : Κ̄Ζ̄ : ⲀⲠΟⲤ : ΟΥⲈⲖⲈΝⲀⲐⲐΙΟΝ ΟΥⲢ   Heb 5:4

ⲢⲰ ⲤΟΚΚⲀ ⲼΟΚΚ ⲈΤⲘⲈΝΚⲈⲢⲀⳠΟ \\ ΤⲖ̣̄

ⲖΙⲖⲰϬⲰⳆ ΟΚΤⲀΚΟⳠⲈΝΚⲰ \\ ⳆⲢⲰΝΝⲀ

ΝΟΝ \\ ⲈΙΚⲀⲢΙⳠⲢⲀ[−]ⳠΟ ΧⲢΙⲤΤΟⲤΙ ΤⲀΚΚΟΝ[Ο]   5

5 ⲀⲢΧΝ̈ⲒⲈ̄Ⲣⲉ̄ⲺⲤⲀⲼⲀ ⲼΟΚ ⲈΤΝΙⳆ ⲘⲈΝΟ

ΝⲀ \\ ΤⲀⲢΓΙⳠⲖⲈ ⲠⲈⲤΟⳠ \\ ⲀΝ ΤΟΤⲀⲘΗ ⲈΙ

ⲢΟΥ Ⲁ̈ⲒⳠΟ ⲐⳠΗ ⲈⳆ ΟΥΝΝⲀⲢⲀⲊΝⳠⲈΝΚⲰ \\

ⳆΓΟΥⲀ ΟΥⲈⳠⲖⲰ ⲠⲈⲤⲈΝ ΚⲈⳠⳠ[Ⲱ] \\Ⲛ̣ ⲈΙⲀ   6

ⲘΗ Ⲓ̈ⲉ̄Ⲣⲉ̄ⲺⲤΟΥ ⲐⳠⳠⲈΝ ΚⲈΤⲀ[ⳠⳠⲈ]Ⲛ̣[(.)]

10 ⲘⲈⳠΧΙⲤⲈⲆⲈΚⲚ̄ ⲠⲀΥΟΥΚΟΥ [ΚⲈΓⲀⲅⲢⳆ(?) \\]

[Ⳇ]ⲤⲚ̄ ΤⲀΝ ΓⳠⲀΝⳆ ΟΥΚⲢ̈ⲒΓΟΥⳠⲰ [± 4].ⲗ̣   7

ⲗ̣ⲉ ⳆΚⲈⳠΙΤΤⲖ̄ⲖⲈΚⲈⳠΚⲀ \\ ⲀⲒⲀ̣Ⲣ̣[−]ⲒⲰ ΤⲀΚ

[Κ]ⲗ ⲀΥΟΥⳠⲐ̄ⲺΚ̄ ⲈΙⲢⲖ̄ΓΙⳠⳠⲈ \\ ΟΥⲗⲰΤⲰ

[..]Κ̣ⲀΤΤⲖ̣̄Ⲁ̣[ⲉ ± 5 [ ]]ⳠⲀⲆⲔⲈⳠⳠⲰⲆⲀⳠ

15 [± 6 Ⳇ].[± 7]ⲩ̣ⲉⳠⲉϬΟΥⲚ

[± 17   ΤΟΤ]ⲗ ⲉⲚⲗ̄Ⳇ   8

[± 22   ]Τ̣ⲉ Τ

— — — — — — — — — — —

(Three lines lost)

(Heb 5:9) . . . became cause of . . ., (10) called by God high priest in accordance with the order (?) of Melchizedek.

Choiak 27, Gospel of John 153 (16:33): "It is these things that I say to you. That you may have peace in me, you have tribulation in the world. But, without worrying, endure, for (?) I have conquered the world." (17:1) And these things Jesus said; raising the pair (?) of his eyes to heaven, he said: "Father, the hour has come; give glory to your Son, that your Son may give glory to you, (2) as you have given him power over all flesh, in order that, as for all you have given him, he may give eternal life to them. (3) And this is the eternal life, to know you . . . and Jesus Christ, whom you sent. (4) And I have given glory to you upon the earth . . . thing . . .

(Heb 5:9) καὶ τελειωθεὶς ἐγένετο πᾶσιν τοῖς ὑπακούουσιν αὐτῷ αἴτιος σωτηρίας αἰωνίου, (10) προσαγορευθεὶς ὑπὸ τοῦ θεοῦ ἀρχιερεὺς κατὰ τὴν τάξιν Μελχισέδεκ.

(Jn 16:33) ταῦτα λελάληκα ὑμῖν· ἵνα ἐν ἐμοὶ εἰρήνην ἔχητε, ἐν τῷ κόσμῳ θλῖψιν ἔχετε· ἀλλὰ θαρσεῖτε, ἐγὼ (γὰρ?) νενίκηκα τὸν κόσμον. (17:1) ταῦτα ἐλάλησεν Ἰησοῦς καὶ ἐπάρας τοὺς ὀφθαλμοὺς αὐτοῦ εἰς τὸν οὐρανὸν εἶπεν· πάτερ, ἐλήλυθεν ἡ ὥρα· δόξασόν σου τὸν υἱόν, ἵνα ὁ υἱός σου δοξάσῃ σε, (2) καθὼς ἔδωκας αὐτῷ ἐξουσίαν πάσης σαρκός, ἵνα πᾶν ὃ δέδωκάς αὐτῷ δώσῃ αὐτοῖς ζωὴν αἰώνιον. (3) αὕτη δέ ἐστιν ἡ αἰώνιος ζωὴ ἵνα γινώσκωσιν σὲ τὸν μόνον ἀληθινὸν θεὸν καὶ ὃν ἀπέστειλας Ἰησοῦν Χριστόν. (4) ἐγώ σε ἐδόξασα ἐπὶ τῆς γῆς τὸ ἔργον τελειώσας ὃ δέδωκάς μοι ἵνα ποιήσω·

16:33 ὑμῖν· ἵνα . . . ἔχητε, ἐν: vd. adn. ad 106.6   γὰρ syˢ saᵐˢˢ aeth arm: om. NA   17:1 ὁ υἱός σου NAᵃᵖᵖ: ὁ υἱός NA

:p̄F̄:

[.]ⲛⲁ̄ ⳟⲟⲩⲣⲓⳝⲁⲣⲁⳝ̄ \\ ⲧⳠⲗⲓⲗⲉ⳿ⲟⲩⲛ ⲁⲣ   Heb 5:10

[ⲭ]ⲏⲓ̄ⲑ̄ⲣⲉⲟ̄ⲥⲁ̄ ⲟⲕⲧⲁⲕⲁ \\ ⲙⲉⲗⲭⲓⲥⲉⲇⲉⲕ̄ⲛ̱

[.]ⲉⲕⲉⲅⲁ̄ⲗⲗⲁⲕⲁ :: ———·····————

[ⲭ]ⲟⲓⳤⲕⲛ̄ : ⲕ̄ⲍ̄ : ⲑ̄ⲩ̄ : ⲧ̄ⲱ̄ⲩ̄ : ⲡ̄ⲛ̄ⲅ̄ [.] ⲉⲛⲛ̄ⲛ̄ⲕⲁ ⲟⲩ[ⲁ]   Jn 16:33

5   ⳡⲓⲗⲗⲉ ⲡⲉⲥⲓⳟⲉⲣⳠ \\ ⲧⲱⲕⲛ̄ⲛⲁⲩⲑ̄ⲕⲁ ⲁⲓ̈ⳤ

ⲕⲟⲛⲕⲟⳠⲗⲱ \\ ⲕⲟⳡⲕⲉ ⲕⲟⲥⲙⲟⲥⲁ̄ ⲙⲁ[ⲓ̈]

ⲕ̄ⲧ̄ⲕⲁ \\ ⲙⲁⲅⲣⲉⲛⲉⲛⲁⳟ ⲧⲟⲩⲗⲗⲓⳤⲁⲛⲁⲥⲱ [\\]

ⲁⲓ̈ ⲕⲟⲥ[ⲙⲟ]ⲥ̣ⲕ ⲉⲥⲕⲓⲥⲉⲥⲛ̄ :: — ⲉⲓⲛⲛ̄ⲕⲁ ⲡⲉⳡ[ⲓ]   17:1

ⳟⲁ̣ⲣ̣[ⲁⲗⲟ]ⲉⲓⲟⲛ ⲓ̈ⲏ̄ⲥⲟⲩⲥⲓ \\ ⲧⲁⲛ ⲙⲁⲫⲛ̄ ⲧⲣ[ⲓ̈]

              [ ]   [_]

10 [ⲕⲁ́ ⳝⲁⲣⲙ]ⲗⲁ̄ⳡⲓⲗⲗⲉ ⲡⲟⲟⳟⳟⲁⲣⲁ ⲡⲉⲥⲥⲛⲁ [\\]

ⲡ̣[ⲁⲡⲟ] ⲧⲁⲣ̣ⲁ̣ⲧ̄ⲗⲟ ⲕ̄ⲣ̄ⲣⲁ ⲉⲛ̄ ⳤⲁⲕⲕⲁ ⳤⲟⲟ[ⲕ]

ⲧⲣ̣ⲉ̣[ⲥ̄]ⲥⲱ \\ ⲉⲛ̄ ⳤⲁⲗ ⲉ̄ⲕⲕⲁ ⳤⲟⲕ ⲧⲣ̄ⲕⲟⲛⲛⲟ[ⳤ \\]

ⳡⲁⲗⲗ ⲙ̄ϣ̄ϣⲁⲛⲛⲁ ⲡⲁⲩⲟⲩⲕⲁ ⲧⲁⲕ[ⲕⲁ] ⲧ̣[ⳓ]

ⲥⲓⲛ ⲕⲉⲗⲗⲱ \\ ⲉⲛ̄ ⲧⲁⲕⲕⲁ ⲧⲓⳟⳟⲓⲥⲛⳤ ⲙ[ϣ̄]

15 ϣⲁⲛⲕⲁ ⲁⲫ⳿ⲓ ⲉⲗⲗⲉⲛ ⲕ̣ⲉⲧⲁⲗⲗⲉⲛⲕⲁ \ⲛ\

ⲧⲉⲕⲕⲁ [ⲧⲓ]ⳟⳟ[ⲓⲕⲟⲛⲛⲟ]ⲁ̣ \\ ⲉⲛ̄ⲙⲟⲛ ⲉⲛ̄   3

ⲛⲁ [ⲁⲫ⳿ⲓ(?) ⲉⲗⲗⲉⲛ ⲕⲉⲧⲁ]ⲗⲗⲉⲛ̣ \ⲛ\ ⲉⲓⲣⲟⲩ

[± 15   ]. ⲉⲓⳤⲣⲓ \\ ⲟⲛ ⲉ[ⲓ]

[ⲧⲣⲉ̄ⲥ̄ⲛ̄ ⲓ̈ⲏ̄ⲥⲟⲩⲥⲓ ⲭⲣⲓⲥ]ⲧⲟⲥⲓⲕⲁ \\ ⲁ̄ⲓ̄ⲟ[ⲛ]   4

                         [_]

20 [ⲉⲕ̄ⲕⲁ ⳤⲟⲕ ⲧⳤ̄ⲥⲉⲥⲛ̄] ⲥⲕ̄ⲧ̄Ⳡⲗⲱ ⳤⲉ[ⲉⲓ-]

[± 15   ]ⲛ̄ⲕ[..]ˌⳡ̣ⲣ[±2]

107

(Jn 17:5) And now, Father, give me glory with you, the glory which I had when I was with you before the world. (6) I manifested your name to men; those whom you gave to me when they (?) came from the world are yours, and you gave them to me, and they kept your word. (7) Now they knew that as for everything which you gave to me < . . . > (8) < . . . > I gave all to them. And they took and truly knew that I came from you, and they believed that you sent me. (9) And I ask concerning them, and I do not ask concerning the world, but concerning those whom you gave to me because they are yours, (10) and all mine are yours, and yours are mine, and in them you gave glory to me. (11) And . . .

(Jn 17:5) καὶ νῦν δόξασόν με σύ, πάτερ, παρὰ σεαυτῷ τῇ δόξῃ ᾗ εἶχον πρὸ τοῦ τὸν κόσμον εἶναι παρὰ σοί. (6) ἐφανέρωσά σου τὸ ὄνομα τοῖς ἀνθρώποις · οὓς ἔδωκάς μοι ἐκ τοῦ κόσμου, σοὶ ἦσαν κἀμοὶ αὐτοὺς ἔδωκας καὶ τὸν λόγον σου τετήρηκαν. (7) νῦν ἔγνωκαν ὅτι πάντα ὅσα δέδωκάς μοι ⟨παρὰ σοῦ εἰσίν · (8) ὅτι τὰ ῥήματα ἃ ἔδωκάς μοι⟩ δέδωκα αὐτοῖς, καὶ αὐτοὶ ἔλαβον καὶ ἔγνωσαν ἀληθῶς ὅτι παρὰ σοῦ ἐξῆλθον, καὶ ἐπίστευσαν ὅτι σύ με ἀπέστειλας. (9) ἐγὼ δὲ περὶ αὐτῶν ἐρωτῶ, οὐ περὶ τοῦ κόσμου ἐρωτῶ ἀλλὰ περὶ ὧν δέδωκάς μοι, ὅτι σοί εἰσιν, (10) καὶ τὰ ἐμὰ πάντα σά ἐστιν καὶ τὰ σὰ ἐμά, καὶ ἐδόξασάς με ἐν αὐτοῖς. (11) καὶ . . .

6 ἀνθρώποις · οὕς: vd. adn. ad 107.4-5   7-8 de verbis per haplographiam omissis vd. adn. ad 107.9 (cf. Metzger 4)   9 δὲ sy^{ps} sa^{ms} aeth arm: om. NA   10 ἐδό-ξασάς με NA^{app}: δεδόξασμαι NA

:p̄z̄:

ⲉ̄ⲗⲟⲛ ⲡⲁⲡⲟ ⲉⲓⲣⲟⲩ ⲁ̈ⲓⲕⲁ ⲋⲟⲕⲟⲩ ⲁⲓⲛⲉⲥⲱ \\   Jn 17:5

ⲉⲓⲣⲓⲱ̄ⲟ̄ⲣⲱ ⲋⲟⲕⲟⲩ ⲕⲟⲥⲙⲟⲥⲁⲝ̄ ⲧⲟⲩⲥⲟⲩ

ⲉⲓⲣⲓ̄ⲟ̄ⲧⲉ̄ⲱ̄ ⲁⲟⲩⲛ ⲕⲟⲩⲥⲥⲓⲕⲁ \\   ⲡⲓⲗⲗⲓⲅⲣⲝ̄   6

ⲧⲓⲉⲉⲓⲥⲉ ⲉⲛ̄ ⲧⲁⲋ̄ⲧ̄ⲕⲁ ⲉⲓⲅⲟⲩⲕⲁ \\   ⲉⲛ̄ ⲕⲟⲥ

5   ⲙⲟⲥⲁⲟ̄ ⲋⲟⲟⲗ ⲁ̈ⲓⲕⲁ ⲁⲉⲛⲉ̄ⲓⲥⲓⲛⲅⲟⲩⲗ ⲉⲛ̄ⲛⲁ

ⲅⲟⲩⲉ̄ⲗⲟ \ ⲧⲉⲕⲕⲟⲛ ⲁ̈ⲓⲕⲁ ⲁⲉⲛⲉ̄ⲁⲣⲁⲗⲏ \\

ⲉ̣ⲛ̄ ⲥⲁⲗⲕⲟⲛ ⲉⲓⲁⲫⲓⲥⲁⲛⲁ \\   ⲉⲗⲗⲱ [ⲉⲓ]ⲁⲥ   7

ⲥⲁⲛⲁ ⲁ̈ⲓⲕⲁ ⲁⲉⲛⲉ̄ⲓⲥⲛ̄ⲝ̄ ⲙⲱ̣̄ⲱ̣[ⲁ]ⲛⲕⲁ \\

ⲕⲉⲗⲗⲱⲕⲁ ⲧⲉⲕⲕⲁ ⲧⲓⲉⲉⲉⲥⲓⲕ̣[ⲁ \\ ⲧⲉⲣⲟⲛ]   8

10   ⲉ̄ⲧⲁⲗⲟ ⲝ̄ⲗⲉⲡⲁⲋ̄ⲋⲁⲗⲗⲟ ⲉⲓⲁⲥⲥⲁⲛ[ⲁ ⲁⲛ]

ⲉⲓⲣⲓⲟ̣̄ⲋ̄ⲟⲩⲛ ⲡⲁⲗⲁ ⲕⲣⲉ̄ⲥⲓⲕⲁ \\   ⲟ[ⲛ ⲡ]ⲓⲥⲧⲉⲩ

[ⲉⲓ]ⲥⲁⲛⲁ \\   ⲉⲛ̄ ⲁ̈ⲓⲕ ⲉⲓⲧⲣⲉⲥⲕⲁ \\   ⲁ̈ⲓⲟⲛ ⲧⲉⲛ   9

ⲋⲟⲩⲣⲓⲝ̄ⲗⲟ ⲥⲉⲛⲛⲉ \\   ⲕⲟⲥⲙⲟⲥⲛ̄ ⲋⲟⲩ

ⲣⲓⲝ̄ⲉⲓⲟⲛ ⲥⲉⲛ[ⲓⲙ]ⲛ̄ⲛⲉ̄ⲗⲟ \\   ⲉⲛ̄ ⲁ̈ⲓⲕⲁ ⲁⲉⲛ

15   ⲉⲓⲥⲓⲛⲅ̣ⲟⲩⲛ ⲋ[ⲟⲩⲣⲓⲝ̄ⲉⲛⲕⲱ \\ ⲉ]ⲛ̄ ⲉ̄ⲛⲉ

ⲣⲁⲛⲛⲟⲋ̄ⲟⲩ[ⲛ \\ ⲁⲛⲛⲁⲅⲟⲩⲗ ⲕⲉⲗⲗⲱ]   10

ⲁⲉ ⲉⲛ̄ⲛⲁⲙ[ⲏ \\ ⲟⲛ ⲉⲛ̄ⲛⲁⲅⲟⲩⲗ ⲁⲛⲛⲁ]

[ⲅ]ⲟⲩⲉ̄ⲗⲟ \\   ⲧⲉⲣ[ⲓ̄ⲟ̄ⲋ̄ⲱⲝ̄ⲉⲓⲟⲛ ⲁ̈ⲓⲕⲁ]

ⲋⲟ[ⲕⲕⲁ ⲁ]ⲉⲛ[ⲓ̄ⲥⲛ̄ⲝ̄ \\ ⲟⲛⲕⲉⲧⲁⲗ ⲕⲟⲥ]   11

(Jn 17:11) . . . I am not in the world, and these are in the world, and I am coming to you, holy Father. Keep them in your name, in order that they may be one, as we are one. (12) And when I was with them in the world, I kept (?) them. In your name, which (?) you gave to me, I kept them, and no one amongst them perished, except the son of perdition, in order that the scripture be fulfilled. (13) And now I am coming to you, and these things I say in the world, in order that they may have my joy fulfilled in themselves. (14) And since (?) I gave them your word, . . . hated them . . .

(Jn 17:11) . . . οὐκέτι εἰμὶ ἐν τῷ κόσμῳ, καὶ οὗτοι ἐν τῷ κόσμῳ εἰσίν, κἀγὼ πρὸς σὲ ἔρχομαι, πάτερ ἅγιε · τήρησον αὐτοὺς ἐν τῷ ὀνόματί σου, ἵνα ὦσιν ἓν καθὼς ἡμεῖς ἕν ἐσμεν. (12) ὅτε ἤμην μετ᾽ αὐτῶν ἐν τῷ κόσμῳ, ἐγὼ ἐτήρουν αὐτούς · ἐν τῷ ὀνόματί σου ᾧ δέδωκάς μοι ἐφύλαξα, καὶ οὐδεὶς ἐξ αὐτῶν ἀπώλετο εἰ μὴ ὁ υἱὸς τῆς ἀπωλείας, ἵνα ἡ γραφὴ πληρωθῇ. (13) νῦν δὲ πρὸς σὲ ἔρχομαι καὶ ταῦτα λαλῶ ἐν τῷ κόσμῳ ἵνα ἔχωσιν τὴν χαρὰν τὴν ἐμὴν πεπληρωμένην ἐν ἑαυτοῖς. (14) ἐγὼ δὲ ἔδωκα αὐτοῖς τὸν λόγον σου καὶ ὁ κόσμος ἐμίσησεν αὐτούς...

11 οὗτοι NA[app]: αὐτοὶ NA   ἔρχομαι, πάτερ: sic, ut videtur, interpres Nub. σου it (a b c e ff²) sy[s] Hil: σου ᾧ δέδωκάς μοι NA   ἕν ἐσμεν: vd. Metzger 5   12 ἐν τῷ κόσμῳ NA[app]: om. NA (cf. Metzger 6)   αὐτούς · ἐν: sic, ut videtur, interpres Nub.   ᾧ NA: οὓς NA[app] (cf. Metzger 7 et vd. adn. ad 108.9)   μοι NA[app]: μοι καὶ NA   14 δὲ ἔδωκα D (cf. sa[ms] aeth arm): δέδωκα NA

: p̄H̄ :

мосаⲭ ⲇоуммінneⲗⲱ \\ ɛінn̄ⲅо[ⲩⲗ]   Jn 17:11

ⲗоn космосаⲭⲗо ⲇоуⲗⲗаnа \\ аïоn

[ɛі]аⲅіⲗⲗɛсn̄ кірɛсn̄ ⲡаⲡа ⲥ̄ⲥа \\ ɛn̄

таⲥсⲗо̄кⲱ тɛкка ɛіаⲫіɛɛсⲱ \\

5   оуɛ̄ріn̄ⲭ ⲇоуккоаⲛⲛо̄ⲭ \\ ɛnna оу[ɛр]

ɛ̄nɛn кɛⲗⲗⲱ \\ космосаⲭ тɛⲇⲗⲇ [аn]   12
     [ ]
ⲇоуɛ̣[n] таукⲗⲱ̄ⲇɛ аïⲗо тɛкка ɛі[ⲇ]

ⲫіɛ[ар]ра \\ ɛіn таⲥсⲗо̄кⲱ ɛn̄ аïка

ⲇɛ[ссіn(?) ɛ]іаⲫісісɛ тɛріⲭ оуɛⲇɛnⲇ[ɛ]

10   ɛ[і]оn ⲇⲇⲡⲡіⲙɛnⲛⲇⲗⲱ \ ⲇⲇⲡⲡіⲇɛn
     [–]
тотⲗɛnкⲱ : : = ⲡартⲭ кіріⲉ̣ік[оn]ⲛо[ⲭ \\]

ɛ̄ⲗоn ɛ̄ⲅⲅіⲗⲗɛⲗо кірɛ \\ ɛіnn̄каɛ̣[і]о̣[n]   13

космосаⲭ ⲡɛсіɛрɛ̄ \\ аn ⲡіскаnɛ к[і]

рⲉ̣̄оⲕⲕⲁ тɛ̣р[іⲭ] ко̣̣ṇкоаⲛⲛо̄ⲭ[. ;] =

15   аïо[n ɛn̄ саⲗка тɛкка] ⲧіɛɛісіоу[.]   14

[± 10   тɛкка] моnɛ[ісn̄ⲭ \\]

- - - - - - - - - - - - - - -

(Three lines lost)

(Jn 17:15) And I do not ask that you take them . . ., but that you keep them from the evil one. (16) And I (*sic*) have not come from the world, just as I have not come from the world. (17) And hallow them in your truth, for (?) your word is the truth. (18) As you sent me into the world, I sent them into the world. (19) And because of them I hallow myself, in order that they too in truth may be hallowed. (20) I do not ask because of these alone, but also because of all who believe in me through their word, (21) in order that they may all be one, as you, Father, are in me, and I am in you, in order that they too may be in us (?), . . . the world . . .

(Jn 17:15) οὐκ ἐρωτῶ ἵνα ἄρῃς αὐτοὺς ἐκ τοῦ κόσμου, ἀλλ᾽ ἵνα τηρήσῃς αὐτοὺς ἐκ τοῦ πονηροῦ. (16) ἐκ τοῦ κόσμου οὐκ εἰσὶν καθὼς ἐγὼ οὐκ εἰμὶ ἐκ τοῦ κόσμου. (17) ἁγίασον αὐτοὺς ἐν τῇ ἀληθείᾳ σου · (καὶ γὰρ?) ὁ λόγος ὁ σὸς ἡ ἀλήθειά ἐστιν. (18) καθὼς ἐμὲ ἀπέστειλας εἰς τὸν κόσμον, κἀγὼ ἀπέστειλα αὐτοὺς εἰς τὸν κόσμον · (19) καὶ ὑπὲρ αὐτῶν ἐγὼ ἁγιάζω ἐμαυτόν, ἵνα ὦσιν καὶ αὐτοὶ ἡγιασμένοι ἐν ἀληθείᾳ. (20) οὐ περὶ τούτων δὲ ἐρωτῶ μόνον, ἀλλὰ καὶ περὶ πάντων τῶν πιστευόντων διὰ τοῦ λόγου αὐτῶν εἰς ἐμέ, (21) ἵνα πάντες ἓν ὦσιν, καθὼς σύ, πάτερ, ἐν ἐμοὶ κἀγὼ ἐν σοί, ἵνα καὶ αὐτοὶ ἐν ἡμῖν ὦσιν, ἵνα ὁ κόσμος . . .

17 σου NA[app]: om. NA   καὶ γὰρ Cramer II 373 sy[ps] aeth arm: om. NA
ἡ Bpc: om. NA   20 πάντων: vd. Metzger 8

:p̄θ̄:

ⲟ̄ⲥ ⲓ ⲉ ⲉⲝⲉ ⲓ ⲟ ⲛ ⲥ ⲉ ⲛ ⲓ ⲙ ⲛ̄ⲛ ⲉ ⲥ ⲱ \\ ⲕ ⲟ ⲥ ⲕ ⲧ̄ ⲕ ⲁ ⲧ	Jn 17:15
ⲧ ⲗ ⲟ̄ ⲧ ⲉ ⲕ ⲕ ⲁ ⲉ ⲓ ⲁ ⲫ ⲓ ⲉ ⲉ ⲓ ⲁ ⲗ̄ⲉ ⲛ ⲕ ⲱ \\ ⲕ ⲟ ⲥ ⲙ [ⲟ]	16
ⲥ ⲓ ⲗ ⲟ ⲙ ⲓ ⲛ ⲛ ⲉ ⲗ ⲱ \\ ⲁ ⲛ ⲛ ⲁ ⲕ ⲟ [ⲥ]	
ⲙ ⲟ ⲥ ⲓ ⲗ ⲟ ⲙ ⲉ ⲛ ⲉ ⲣ ⲓ ⲕ ⲉ ⲗ ⲗ ⲱ \\ ⲉ ⲛ̄ⲛ [ⲁ]	17
5 ⲝ̄ⲗ ⲉ ⲗ ⲟ ⲕ ⲟ ⲉ ⲓ ⲟ ⲛ ⲧ ⲉ ⲕ ⲕ ⲁ ⲥ ⲓ ⲥ ⲥ ⲁ ⲅ ⲁ ⲣ ⲉ ⲱ \\	
ⲉ ⲛ̄ⲛ ⲁ ⲥ ⲁ ⲗ ⲧ̄ⲥ ⲓ ⲛ ⲉ ⲛ̄ⲛ ⲁ ⲥ ⲛ̄ \\ ⲝ̄ⲗ ⲉ ⲗ ⲕ ⲟ ⲥ ⲙ ⲟ	18
[ⲥ] ⲗ ⲝ̄ⲅ ⲓ ⲁ ⲁ ⲓ̈ ⲕ ⲉ ⲓ ⲧ ⲣ ⲉ̄ ⲥ ⲓ ⲛ ⲕ ⲉ ⲗ ⲗ ⲱ \\ ⲁ ⲓ̈ ⲧ ⲉ ⲕ ⲕ ⲁ	
ⲕ ⲟ ⲥ ⲙ ⲟ ⲥ ⲗ ⲝ̄ⲅ ⲓ ⲁ ⲉ ⲓ ⲧ ⲁ ⲥ ⲥ ⲉ \\ⲛ\\ ⲧ ⲉ ⲛ [ⲉ] ⲟ ⲩ ⲣ ⲓ ⲝ̄	19
ⲙ ⲟ ⲛ ⲁ ⲓ̈ ⲁ ⲓ̈ ⲕ ⲟ ⲛ ⲟ ⲥ̄ⲧ̄ⲥ ⲁ ⲥ̄ ⲣ ⲉ ⲥ ⲱ [\\ ⲧ ⲉ ⲕ] ⲕ̣ ⲉ	
10 ⲧ ⲁ ⲗ ⲝ̄ⲗ ⲉ ⲗ ⲟ ⲥ̄ⲧ̄ⲥ ⲁ̣ ⲥ̄ ⲣ ⲉ ⲓ ⲛ ⲓ̄ [ⲗ ⲟ] ⲩ̣ [ⲕ ⲕ] ⲟ ⲁ ⲛ	
ⲛ ⲟ ⲝ̄ [\\] ⲉ ⲓ ⲛ ⲗ ⲟ̣ ⲩ ⲟ ⲩ ⲧ ⲅ ⲟ ⲩ ⲛ ⲉ ⲟ ⲩ ⲣ [ⲓ] ⲝ̄ ⲥ ⲉ ⲛ ⲓ	20
ⲙ̣ [ⲓ] ⲛ̣ ⲛ ⲉ ⲗ ⲟ \\ ⲧ ⲉ ⲛ ⲥ ⲁ ⲗ ⲗ ⲱ ⲕ ⲱ ⲁ̣ ⲓ̈ ⲅ ⲓ ⲁ ⲡ ⲥ̄	
ⲧ ⲉ ⲩ ⲉ ⲓ ⲣ̣ ⲁ ⲙ ⲓ ⳝ ⳝ ⲁ ⲛ ⲅ ⲟ ⲩ ⲛ ⲉ ⲟ ⲩ ⲣ ⲓ ⲝ̄ ⲕ ⲉ	
ⲧ ⲁ ⲗ ⲉ ⲛ ⲕ̣ ⲱ \\ ⲕ ⲉ ⲗ ⲗ ⲱ ⲟ ⲩ ⲉ̄ ⲣ ⲓ ⲛ ⲝ̄ ⲗ ⲟ ⲩ ⲕ	21
15 ⲕ ⲟ ⲗ̣ ⲛ ⲛ ⲟ ⲝ̄ ⲉ̄ ⲣ ⲟ̣ [ⲩ ⲡ ⲁ ⲡ ⲟ ⲉ ⲛ̄ⲛ ⲁ] ⲁ̣ ⲓ̈ ⲝ̄ \\ ⲁ ⲛ	
ⲛ̣ ⲁ ⲉ ⲓ ⲟ ⲛ ⲉ [ⲓ ⲣ ⲓ ⲝ̄ ⲉ̄ ⲛ ⲉ ⲛ ⲕ ⲉ ⲗ ⲗ ⲱ \\] ⲧ ⲉ ⲕ	
[ⲕ ⲉ ⲧ ⲁ ⲗ] ⲉ ⲓ ⲣ ⲓ̣ [ⲝ̄ ⲉ ⲛ̄ⲕ ⲟ ⲗ ⲛ ⲛ ⲟ ⲝ̄ \\ ⲕ ⲟ ⲥ ⲙ ⲟ ⲥ ⲓ] ⲗ̣	

— — — — — — — — —

(Two lines lost)

(Jn 17:22) . . . I gave to them, in order that they might be one, as we are one, (23) both you in me and I in them, in order that what pertains to these people's being one (?) may be fulfilled, in order that the world may know that you sent me, and you loved them as you loved me. (24) Father, as for the ones you gave me, I wish that those will be with me in my places, in order that they may see the glory which you gave to me, because (?) you loved me before the foundation of the world, (25) just Father, and the world did not know you, but I knew you. And these too knew that you sent me. (26) . . . "

(Jn 17:22) . . . δέδωκα αὐτοῖς, ἵνα ὦσιν ἓν καθὼς ἡμεῖς ἕν ἐσμεν, (23) ἐγὼ ἐν αὐτοῖς καὶ σὺ ἐν ἐμοί, ἵνα ὦσιν τετελειωμένοι εἰς ἕν, ἵνα γινώσκῃ ὁ κόσμος ὅτι σύ με ἀπέστειλας καὶ ἠγάπησας αὐτοὺς καθὼς ἐμὲ ἠγάπησας. (24) πάτερ, οὓς δέδωκάς μοι, θέλω ἵνα ὅπου εἰμὶ ἐγὼ κἀκεῖνοι ὦσιν μετ' ἐμοῦ, ἵνα θεωρῶσιν τὴν δόξαν ἣν δέδωκάς μοι ὅτι ἠγάπησάς με πρὸ καταβολῆς κόσμου. (25) πάτερ δίκαιε, καὶ ὁ κόσμος σε οὐκ ἔγνω, ἐγὼ δέ σε ἔγνων, καὶ οὗτοι ἔγνωσαν ὅτι σύ με ἀπέστειλας. (26) . . .

22 ἐσμεν NA^{app}: om. NA (cf. Metzger 9)   24 οὓς NA^{app}: ὃ NA   τὴν δόξαν
NA^{app}: τὴν δόξαν τὴν ἐμήν NA

:p̄ι̅ [.]

τι6]/6ιce \\ ογ6ρ6ινλ̅ λογκκολνν[ολ̅ \\ 6ν]	Jn 17:22
ν̣λ ογ6ρ̅ν6ν κ6λλω \\ 6ιλλ̣6 [λϊλ̅ λϊον]	23
[τ]6ρι̅λ̅ \\ 6ν̅νι ογ6ρ6ιννι̣ [κιρι̣λ̅ρ6ι]	
[ν]ι̣λ λογκκοννολ̅ \\ κοcμοcι̣ λ̣[κκον]	
5 νολ̅ 6ιν λϊκ 6ιτρ6κλ \\ τ6κκον [ον6λ]	
ρλλη \\ λϊκ ον6cιν κ6λλω \\ πλπο 6ν̅^[_]	24
λϊκλ λ6ν6̣ιcινκλ λολλιμμ6 \\ λν	
λογ[τ6]γουλλω μινινγουνλ λϊλλ	
λο[γλλ6]λ̣κλ \\ λ̅οκογ 6ιν λϊκλ λιc	
10 cι̣ν̣κ̣λ λ̅λκκολννολ̅ \\ κοcμοcιν	
ογκογρτλο̅ τογcογ λϊκ ον!̣[cνλ̅c]!̣[ν(?)]	
πλπλ τι6κλττλ κοcμ[οc(ι)λλον 6κ̅]	25
λ̅ριμ6νλλω \\ λϊον 6κ̅ [λ̅ριc6 \\ 6ιν̅ν̅]	
γουλκ6[τλλλ66ιο]ν̣ 6ιλ[ccλνλ \\]	
15 6ιν [λϊκ 6ιτρ6cκλ	26

- - - - - - - - - - - - -

(Four lines lost)

(Heb 9:1) . . . had service ordinances and a holy place of the earth. (2) For the . . . tabernacle was set up, in which were the lampstand and the table and the bread displays, and this is named the Holy. (3) And that which comes after veil two is called the tabernacle which is the Holy of Holies, (4) having the golden incense-altar and the [ark] of the covenant, which they covered on all sides [with] gold, in which were the golden jar (?), manna being within (?) . . .

(Heb 9:1) Εἶχε μὲν οὖν [καὶ] ἡ πρώτη δικαιώματα λατρείας τό τε ἅγιον κοσμικόν. (2) σκηνὴ γὰρ κατεσκευάσθη ἡ πρώτη ἐν ᾗ ἥ τε λυχνία καὶ ἡ τράπεζα καὶ ἡ πρόθεσις τῶν ἄρτων, ἥτις λέγεται Ἁγία · (3) μετὰ δὲ τὸ δεύτερον καταπέτασμα σκηνὴ ἡ λεγομένη Ἁγία Ἁγίων, 4) χρυσοῦν ἔχουσα θυμιατήριον καὶ τὴν κιβωτὸν τῆς διαθήκης περικεκαλυμμένην πάντοθεν χρυσίῳ, ἐν ᾗ στάμνος χρυσῆ ἔχουσα τὸ μάννα . . .

---

1 [καὶ]: num in exemplari incertum   2, 3 Ἁγία: sic interpres Nub. (vd. adn. ad 111.6)

[̄ ̄ ̄]
[⋮ ρ ɪ]λ :

[ⲕⲟⲛⲉ ɪ] ϛⲛⲁ̄ ⲋⲁⲗⲗⲟⲩ ⲧ ɪⲋ ⲕⲁⲛⲉⲛ ɪ ⲅⲟⲩ [ⲕⲁ \\]   Heb 9:1

[ⲥⲕ̄ⲧ̄ⲛ] ⲁ̄ⲉ ɪⲟⲛ ⲁⲟⲩⲧⲉ ⲥ ɪ ⲥⲥ ɪ ⲕⲁ \\ ⲥⲁ [ⲩⲉ ɪ]   2

[ρⲟⲩ   4-5   ] ⲗⲁⲡⲡⲁ ⲁⲕⲁⲗⲕⲧⲁⲕⲁ ρ ̣ⲁ [ⲥⲛ̄ \\]

[ⲧⲁ ρ ɪ] ⲗⲁ̣ ⲗ ɪ ⲭⲭ ɪ ⲛⲁ ɪ ⲛⲁⲉ \\ ⲧ ρⲁ̄ⲡ ɪ ⲥ ɪ ⲗⲁ [ⲉ]

ⲅⲟⲩⲗ
5 [ⲡⲁ ρ] ⲟⲩ ⲟⲩⲥⲕⲟⲩ ρ ⲧⲛ̄ⲁ̣ⲉ ⲕⲉⲛⲛⲁ ⲁⲟⲩ

ⲥ̄ⲥⲁⲛ \\ ⲉ ɪ ⲛⲁⲉ ⲥ̄ⲥⲥⲁⲗⲟ ⲡⲉⲥⲧⲁⲕⲟⲛⲁ \\

ⲕⲁⲧⲁⲡⲉⲧⲁⲥⲙⲁ ⲟⲩⲟⲩⲕⲁⲗ ̣ⲟ ⲡⲁⲗⲗ   3

ⲕ ɪ ⲗⲗⲟⲛ \\ ⲥⲁⲩⲉ ɪ ρⲁ ⲥ̄ⲥ̄ⲥ [ɪ ⲅⲟⲩ] ⲛⲁ

ⲥ̄ⲥ̄ⲥⲁⲁ̄ⲗⲟ ⲟⲕⲧⲁⲕⲛⲁ̄ \\ ⲕ [ⲟ] ⲛ̣ [ⲋ ɪ] ⲗ   4

10 ⲥⲁ [ⲡ] ⲕ ̣ⲟ̣ ⲧ ɪ ⲙ ɪ ⲁ̄ⲧ ρ̄ⲕⲁ \\ ⲟ̄ⲛ ⲁ ɪ ⲅ ̣ρ ⲧⲛ̄

[± 6] . [ⲟ] ⲩ̣ ⲧⲁⲡⲁ ⲙ ⳬⳬⲁⲛⲛⲟ ⲥⲁ

[ⲡ(ɪ)- ± 7] ⲡ ɪ ⲅ ɪ ⲥⲥⲁⲛⲕⲁ \\ ⲧⲁ ρ ɪ

[_]
[ⲁ̄ ⲥⲁⲡⲕⲟ] ⲉ̣ⲙⲉ ⲙⲁⲛⲛⲁⲛ ⲁⲩⲁ̄ ⲁⲁ

[± 17   ] .ⲁⲟⲩ

15 [± 19   ] .

‒ ‒ ‒ ‒ ‒ ‒ ‒ ‒ ‒ ‒ ‒ ‒ ‒

(Probably three lines lost)

(Heb 9:5)... concerning... it is not possible to speak individually.

Choiak 28, Matthew 3 (1:18): Thus is the birth of God. End: Until he called (his name) Jesus. It is written (in) Choiak 24.

Choiak 29, Apostle (Gal 4:4): And in the fulness of the times God sent his Son, born of a virgin, coming under the law, (5) in order that he might redeem those who are under the law, in order that they might receive the sonship of God. (6) Because you are sons of God, he sent the Spirit of his Son to our (?) hearts, crying (?)... (7)... you are...

(Heb 9:5)... περὶ ὧν οὐκ ἔστιν νῦν λέγειν κατὰ μέρος.

(Mt 1:18-25) τοῦ δὲ Ἰησοῦ Χριστοῦ ἡ γένεσις οὕτως ἦν—ἕως οὗ—ἐκάλεσεν—Ἰησοῦν. (Vd. adn. ad 112.3-5)

(Gal 4:4) ὅτε δὲ ἦλθεν τὸ πλήρωμα τοῦ χρόνου, ἐξαπέστειλεν ὁ θεὸς τὸν υἱὸν αὐτοῦ, γενόμενον ἐκ γυναικός, γενόμενον ὑπὸ νόμον, (5) ἵνα τοὺς ὑπὸ νόμον ἐξαγοράσῃ, ἵνα τὴν υἱοθεσίαν ἀπολάβωμεν. (6) ὅτι δέ ἐστε υἱοὶ τοῦ θεοῦ, ἐξαπέστειλεν τὸ πνεῦμα τοῦ υἱοῦ αὐτοῦ εἰς τὰς καρδίας ἡμῶν (?) κρᾶζον· ἀββὰ ὁ πατήρ. (7) ὥστε οὐκέτι εἶ...

4:5 τὴν υἱοθεσίαν: "adoptationem dei" (interpres Nub. liberior)   ἀπολάβωμεν: "recipiant" (vd. adn. ad 112.10-11)   6 υἱοὶ τοῦ θεοῦ: vd. Metzger 10   ἐξαπέστειλεν NA[app]: ἐξαπέστειλεν ὁ θεός NA (cf. Metzger 11)   ἡμῶν NA: aut ὑμῶν NA[app] (vd. adn. ad 112.12)

[————]
: ⲣⲓⲃ [:]

ϭⲟⲩⲣⲓⲕⲁ ⲙⲓⲛⲁⲓ ⲙⲛ̄ⲁⲓⲗⲟ ⲡⲉⲥⲓⲛⲁ	Heb 9:5
ⲇⲟⲩⲙⲙⲉⲛⲉⲥⲥⲛ̄ : : ——— · · · · · ——	
ⲭⲟⲓⲍ̄ⲕⲛ̄ : ⲕ̄ⲏ̄ : ⲙⲁⲧ : ⲅ̄ : ⲉⲓⲕⲁⲣⲁⲗⲟ	Mt 1:18
[ⲧ]ⲗ̄ⲗ̄ⲛ̄ ⲣ̄ⲕⲁⲛⲉⲗ : ⲧⲉ ⲓ̄ⲏ̄ⲥⲟⲩⲥⲓⲍ̄ ⲟ̄ⲕⲉⲛ	25
5 ⲡⲁⲩⲟⲩⲕⲁ : : ⲭⲟⲓⲍ̄ⲕⲛ̄ : : ⲕ̄ⲁ̄ : : ⲡⲁⲣ̄ : : —	
———————— · · · · · ———— · · · · · —	
ⲭⲟⲓⲍ̄ⲕⲛ̄ : ⲕ̄ⲑ̄ : ⲍ̄ⲡⲟⲥ : ⲧⲁⲩⲟⲩⲕⲅⲟⲩⲛ ⲉⲓ	Gal 4:4
ⲗⲁⲛⲧⲉⲗⲟⲑⲓⲟⲛ ⲧⲗ̄ⲗ̄ ⲧⲁⲛ ⲧⲟⲧⲕⲁ ⲉⲓⲧⲣ̄	
ⲥⲛ̄ \\ ⲡⲁⲣⲑⲉⲛⲟⲥⲗ̄ⲟ̄ ⲟⲩⲛⲛⲟⲩⲧⲁⲕⲁ \\ ⲧⲉ	
ⲁⲛ̄ ⲧⲁⲩⲱ̄ ⲧⲟⲣⲁ \\ ⲧⲉⲁⲛ̄ ⲧⲁⲩⲱ̄ ⲁⲗⲗⲟⲩⲕ[ⲁ]	5
10 ϭⲁⲛⲟ̄ⲥⲓⲉⲉⲥⲁ \\ ⲧⲗ̄ⲗⲓⲛ ⲧⲟⲧⲕⲁⲛⲉⲕ ⲉⲧ	
ⲕⲟⲗⲛⲛⲟⲍ̄ \\ ⲧⲗ̄ⲗⲛ̄ ⲧⲟⲩⲫⲉⲅⲟⲩⲉ̄ⲥⲓⲛ [ⲉⲛ̄]	6
ⲛⲟⲥⲓⲛ \\ ⲧⲁⲛ ⲧⲟⲧⲛ̄ ⲥⲉⲩⲁⲣⲧⲓⲕⲁⲗⲟ ⲉ̣[ⲛ]	
ⲍ̄ⲉⲓⲗⲟⲩⲗⲁⲅⲓⲁ ⲉⲓⲧ[ⲣ̄]ⲥ̣[ⲛ]ⲁ̄ \\ ⲉⲓⲛⲧ[±3]	
ⲕⲣⲟⲩⲗ[· ·] · · · · [± 15]	7
15 ⲉⲛ̄ . [	

– — – — – — – — – — – — – —

(Three lines lost)

113

(Mt 2:1) ... when (Jesus) was born in Bethlehem of Judaea, in the days of Herod the king, behold, magi coming from the east arrived in Jerusalem, (2) saying: "Where is the king of the Jews who has been born? For seeing his star in the east, we came to worship him." (3) And Herod the king, when he heard, was disturbed, and all Jerusalem with him. (4) And assembling (?) all the high priests and the scribes of the people, he asked them: "Where is Christ born?" (5) And they said to him: "In Bethlehem of Judaea. For thus it was written ... "

(Mt 2:1) (τοῦ δὲ Ἰησοῦ) γεννηθέντος ἐν Βηθλέεμ τῆς Ἰουδαίας ἐν ἡμέραις Ἡρῴδου τοῦ βασιλέως, ἰδοὺ μάγοι ἀπὸ ἀνατολῶν παρεγένοντο εἰς Ἱεροσόλυμα (2) λέγοντες· ποῦ ἐστιν ὁ τεχθεὶς βασιλεὺς τῶν Ἰουδαίων; εἴδομεν γὰρ αὐτοῦ τὸν ἀστέρα ἐν τῇ ἀνατολῇ καὶ ἤλθομεν προσκυνῆσαι αὐτῷ. (3) ἀκούσας δὲ ὁ βασιλεὺς Ἡρῴδης ἐταράχθη καὶ πᾶσα Ἱεροσόλυμα μετ' αὐτοῦ, (4) καὶ συναγαγὼν πάντας τοὺς ἀρχιερεῖς καὶ γραμματεῖς τοῦ λαοῦ ἐπυνθάνετο παρ' αὐτῶν· ποῦ ὁ Χριστὸς γεννᾶται; (5) οἱ δὲ εἶπαν αὐτῷ· ἐν Βηθλέεμ τῆς Ἰουδαίας· οὕτως γὰρ γέγραπται...

ρ ι γ :

[ο] γ ν ν ο γ τ ⲁ κ ο ν   β η ⲑ ⲗ ⲉ̅ μ η   ϊ ο γ ⲇ ⲇ ι ⲁ ⲛ̣   Mt 2:1

ν ο \\ ⲏ̅ ρ ω ⲇ η   ο γ ρ ο γ ν ⲁ   ο γ κ ρ ϊ γ ο γ λ ω \\ [ε ι ⲥ]

ⲥ ⲛ̅   ⲇ ο γ ⲁ ρ ϊ γ ο γ ⲗ   μ ⲁ ⲫ ⲁ ⲗ ο ⲥ κ ⲁ̅ ⲟ   τ ⲁ ρ ⲁ   [\\ (?)]

ϊ ⲑ̅ ρ ο γ ⲥ ⲁ ⲗ μ ι ⲟ̅   κ ι ⲥ ⲁ ν ⲁ   π ε ⲥ ρ ⲝ̅ γ ο γ [ⲑ̅]   2

5   ε ι ν ι ⲁ \\ ⲧ̅ ⲗ ο   π ι ν ⲁ   ϊ ο γ ⲇ ⲇ ι ο ⲥ ⲅ ο γ ν   ο γ

ρ ο γ ο γ   ο γ ν ν ο γ τ ⲁ κ ο ⲗ \\ τ ⲁ ν   ο γ ε ι φ

ⲉ ι κ ⲁ   μ ⲁ ⲫ ⲁ ⲗ ο ⲥ κ ι ⲗ ο   ⳝ ⲁ ⲥ ⲛ̅   κ ⲁ ⲥ ⲥ ο

ⲥ ι ν   τ ⲁ κ κ ⲁ   ⲇ ο γ κ ο γ ν ο γ ⲝ̅ \\ ⲏ̅ ρ ω ⲇ η   3

ο γ ρ ο γ ε ⲝ̅ ⲗ ο ν   ο γ ⲁ ⲅ ρ ε ν   π ⲁ ν ν ι ⲥ ⲛ̅ ⲝ̅ \\

10   [ϊ] ⲑ̅ ρ ο γ ⲥ ⲁ ⲗ μ η   ο γ ⲁ τ τ ο ⲗ ⲗ ο ν   τ ⲁ ⲇ

ⲇ ⲗ \\ ⲁ ρ ⲭ η ϊ ⲑ̅ ρ ε ⲟ̅ ⲥ ⲁ   μ ⲟ̅ ⲫ ⲁ ν ⲅ ο γ ⲗ   4

[ⲇ] ε   κ ⲛ̅ τ ⲛ̅   ο γ ρ ⲁ ν ι ⲅ ο γ ⲗ ⲇ ⲉ κ ⲉ ⲗ ⲅ ο γ κ ο ν \\

[τ ⲏ̅] μ ι ⲅ ⲁ ρ ⲁ   [τ] ⲉ̣ [κ] κ ⲁ   ⲑ̅ ⲅ ι ⲇ ⲉ ι ⲥ ⲛ̅ ⲝ̅   ⲉ ι ⲥ ⲁ̅ ⲟ

[ⲭ ρ ι ⲥ τ ο ⲥ ι   ο γ ν ν ο γ] τ ⲁ κ ο ν ⲁ̣ ⲝ̅ \\ τ ⲑ̅ ρ ο ν   5

15   [τ ⲁ ⲇ ⲅ ι ⲁ   π ⲉ ⲥ ⲥ ⲁ ν ⲁ \\ β η ⲑ ⲗ ⲉ̅ μ] ⲏ̣   ϊ ο γ ⲇ ⲇ ι

[ⲇ ν ν ο \\ ⲉ ι κ ⲁ ρ ι ⲅ ρ ⲝ̅ ⲗ ο   π ⲁ ρ τ] ⲗ / [κ ι ⲥ ⲛ̅ ⲁ̅ ⲥ ⲛ̅ (?)

— — — — — — — — — — — — — — — —

(Three lines lost)

114

(Mt 2:6) . . . who will shepherd my people Israel. (7) Herod . . . the magi . . . the time . . . (8) Sending them to Bethlehem, he said: "Go (?) and enquire . . . concerning the child; and when you find him, return and tell me, in order that I too may go and bring (?) . . . " (9) And when they heard the king, they went. And behold, the star which they saw in the east, going in their midst, took them, until, being [over] the lying place of the child, it remained standing overhead. (10) And when they saw the star, in a great joy they rejoiced. (11) . . .

(Mt 2:6) . . . ὅστις ποιμανεῖ τὸν λαόν μου τὸν Ἰσραήλ. (7) τότε Ἡρῴδης λάθρᾳ καλέσας τοὺς μάγους ἠκρίβωσεν παρ' αὐτῶν τὸν χρόνον τοῦ φαινομένου ἀστέρος, (8) καὶ πέμψας αὐτοὺς εἰς Βηθλέεμ εἶπεν · πορευθέντες ἐξετάσατε ἀκριβῶς περὶ τοῦ παιδίου · ἐπὰν δὲ εὕρητε, ἀπαγγείλατέ μοι, ὅπως κἀγὼ ἐλθὼν προσκυνήσω αὐτῷ. (9) οἱ δὲ ἀκούσαντες τοῦ βασιλέως ἐπορεύθησαν καὶ ἰδοὺ ὁ ἀστήρ, ὃν εἶδον ἐν τῇ ἀνατολῇ, προῆγεν αὐτούς, ἕως ἐλθὼν ἐστάθη ἐπάνω οὗ ἦν τὸ παιδίον. (10) ἰδόντες δὲ τὸν ἀστέρα ἐχάρησαν χαρὰν μεγάλην σφόδρα. (11) . . .

[: p̄ ιλ :]

[ ]	Mt 2:6
[ε]γλλιλ λ[ν κπ̄τογ ϊcρλ̄η̄λικλ \\ η̄ρω]	7
[λ]η λογλρ[ϊγογκλ ± 13]	
[..]γνι.[± 18]	
5 [τ]λγογκκλ [\\ βθλε̄μηλλγιλ τεκ]	8
ειτλριc[λ πε]c̣[cνλ̄ \\ 60ρλ(?) τοτν̄ 60γ]	
ρικλ πλ660νν̣[λcω ± 5 \\ τλκ]	
ε̄λεννον γπρ̄τλ̣ [λϊγιλ πεc(?)λνλ]	
cω [\\] λ̣ϊκετλλ κιλ̣ [± 9]	
10 ετ̣[κοϊο̄λ(?) \\ τερον ογρογκ ογλγρεν]	9
6ωρicλ̣[νλ \\ ειc(?) ογειφ6ιλ μλϣλλ]	
οcκλ[ο̄ c̄λ̄]c̣[λ]ν̣ν[ον τ]εριο̄ κ̣[ιλ̄ τεκ]	
λ̄ρ̣ιc̣ν̣λ \\ τοτν̄ κενγογλκ[± 3]	
πιλ οκιμε66λ cον6εν [πλγογκλ]	
15 ογειφ6ικλ cλλενη̣[ον πιcκλνε(?)]	10
λλγ[ε̄λο πιccιcλνλ(?)	11

– – – – – – – – – – –

(Probably four lines lost)

(Mt 2:11-12) . . .

Choiak 30, Apostle (Rom 8:3): . . . sending his Son in the likeness of the flesh of sin, for sin he condemned sin in the flesh, (4) in order that the justification of the law might be fulfilled in us, who do not [walk *aut sim.*] according to flesh, but according to spirit. (5) For those who are . . . flesh think things of flesh, but those of spirit things of spirit. (6) And (?) the thought of flesh is death, but the thought of spirit . . . (7) . . . of flesh . . .

(Mt 2:11-12) . . . καὶ χρηματισθέντες κατ' ὄναρ μὴ ἀνακάμψαι πρὸς Ἡρώ-δην, δι' ἄλλης ὁδοῦ ἀνεχώρησαν εἰς τὴν χώραν αὐτῶν.

(Rom 8:3) . . . τὸν ἑαυτοῦ υἱὸν πέμψας ἐν ὁμοιώματι σαρκὸς ἁμαρ-τίας περὶ ἁμαρτίας κατέκρινεν τὴν ἁμαρτίαν ἐν τῇ σαρκί, (4) ἵνα τὸ δικαίωμα τοῦ νόμου πληρωθῇ ἐν ἡμῖν τοῖς μὴ κατὰ σάρκα περιπατοῦσιν ἀλλὰ κατὰ πνεῦμα. (5) οἱ γὰρ κατὰ σάρκα ὄντες τὰ τῆς σαρκὸς φρονοῦσιν, οἱ δὲ κατὰ πνεῦμα τὰ τοῦ πνεύματος. (6) τὸ δὲ (?) φρόνημα τῆς σαρκὸς θά-νατος, τὸ δὲ φρόνημα τοῦ πνεύματος ζωὴ καὶ εἰρήνη · (7) διότι τὸ φρό-νημα τῆς σαρκὸς . . .

8:3 περὶ sy bo^{mss} Or: καὶ περὶ NA   6 δὲ¹ 1908 aeth: γὰρ NA

[: p̄ ι ε :]

[ ]	Mt 2:11
[± 18] ọoγαnn[1-2]	12
[± 19] εⲭ \\ ⲧ̄ⲁ[1-2]	
[± 19] . εϲε . [1-2]	

├————————{

5 [ⲭⲟⲓⲭⲕⲛ̄ : ⲭ : ⲭⲡⲟⲥ : ⲧⲁ]ⲛ ⲧⲟⲧⲕⲁ   Rom 8:3

[ⲥⲁⲡⲉⲛ ⲅⲁⲁⲛ̄ ⲕⲟⲗⲁⲧ(?)ⲗ]ⲭ̣ ⲟⲩⲧⲟⲩⲣⲉ ⲓⲧⲣⲁ \\

[ⲥⲁⲡⲉⲗⲁⲱ(?) ⲅⲁⲁⲗⲟ̄ ⲥ]ⲁⲡⲉⲕⲁ ⲙⲓⲁⲁⲟⲛ

[± 3   ⲉⲣⲓⲭ ⲧⲉⲁⲛ̄] ⲧ̣ⲓ6ⲕⲁⲛⲉⲁ ⲕⲓⲣ!ⲥ̣!   4

[ⲕⲟⲛⲛⲟⲭ \\ ⲅⲁⲁⲛ̄ ⲕⲉⲅⲁ]ⲅⲡⲭ 6[..].ⲣⲙⲓ

10 [ⲛⲓⲗ \\ ⲥⲉⲩⲁⲣⲧⲛ̄ ⲕⲉⲅⲁⲅⲡⲭⲉ]ⲛ̣ⲕⲱ \\

[ⲅⲁⲗ.(.)] ⲁⲟⲩⲗⲧ̣ọ[ⲩⲥ]ⲥ̣!ⲛ [ⲅⲁⲁⲛ̄ ⲥ̣]ⲉⲉⲓⲅⲟⲩ   5

[ⲕⲁ ⲕⲟ]ⲩⲣⲕⲟⲩ6ⲓⲕ[ⲓ(?)]ⲛⲛⲁⲥⲓ̣ⲛ [\\ ⲥⲉ]ⲩⲁⲣⲧⲛ̄

[ⲅⲟⲩⲗⲟⲛ ⲥ]ⲉⲩⲁⲣⲧⲛ̄ⲕⲁ \\ ⲅⲁⲁⲛ̄ ⲕⲟⲩⲣⲕⲓ   6

[ⲟⲛ(?) ⲁⲓⲭⲣⲁⲥ]!ⲛ \\ ⲥⲉⲩⲁⲣⲧⲛ̄ ⲕⲟⲩⲣⲕⲓⲟⲛ

15 [± 9   .... ⲅⲁ]ⲁⲛ̄   7

[± 23   ]ⲛ̣

– – – – – – – – – – – – – –

(Several lines lost)

COMMENTARY

100

1 *e*[*isn̄?*] G., but cf. *eissn̄* (= ἰδού) in NI 78/35 i 19 (Ps 86[87]:4); see also below, 113.2-3n.

4 *emmanouêla* G. (*emmanouêlā* in Index, 127).

5 *eiṣn* G I can discern a faint trace of the stroke over *n*.

6 *īōsêphieion*: The letter phi is filled with red ink.

8 *ṭ*[. *es*]*n̄* G. For *ṭ*[*rēs*]*n̄* see §§135.1, 153 Anm., 238, and cf. BanG III 5.1.

8-9 *par*[*the*]*noska* G.

9 *e*]*ṇarisna* ∖ *takkoṇ* G. For *-on̄* see NON VIII 59.

10 [*e*]*iāṛilgir-* G. (for the form see BanG III 3.3.3).

10-11 *ṅ*[*a* . . . .?] *tk̄kn̄ṇ*[. . . . *ou*]*nṇn̄* ∖ *ta*[*n tagˢkon?*] G. (*tagˢkon* is a misprint). The word *ou*]*nṇn̄*, if correctly read and restored, is subjunctive and need not be followed by the conjunction *-on*; therefore [*taṅˢka*], first proposed by Schäfer-Schmidt, *Handschriften* 603, should be read (cf. above, line 3). The clause as a whole may have run as follows: *tan ṅ*[*akka*] *tk̄kn̄ṇo* [*eīou*]*nṇn̄* ∖ *taṅ* [*taṅˢka*] *īēsou*[*siā ōke*]*n pauouka*, "until, when she conceived and bore her son as is proper, he called his name Jesus." For *tk̄kn̄ṇo* cf. St. 13.2-3 and perhaps 102.1. *eī-* is here supplied exempli gratia in the sense of "conceive"; cf. M. 6.7 *eīkn̄ kog̊r-* "seed of conception"; for the construction see §300. If the Greek model had πρωτότοκον, *tk̄kn̄ṇo* can hardly be considered to render it. Note that the translator took ἔτεκεν and ἐκάλεσεν as dependent upon ἕως; by using the subjunctive *ou*]*nṇn̄* he seems to have implied a change of subject: cf. §§332, 334, and Abel 42.

12 *pauouka* ∖ G.

13 [*choiākn̄* : *kē*]: *apos.*ᵗ G. Of *choiākn̄*, traces remain of *i* and

the following supraliteral stroke. Both of the double dots after *apos*^t
were read by Schäfer-Schmidt, *Handschriften* 603, but I can discern
only the lower. There is a lacuna above the *a* in *apos*^t, and it may
have held a stroke; the scribe's practice seems to vary with this word:
cf. 105.1 *apos*^t and 112.6 *āpos*^t.

14 [*go*]*ueke* ＼ ? [*t*]*auka* G.

15 *eṇo*[*u*]*lgourk*[. .]*sṇ* G. Beginning in the preceding line, Abel
read [*t*]*auk·a miššann*[*o* . . . .]*eṅ·*[*u*]*lg·ur·ka*[·]*sn ke*[*l·lô*] (39), following autoptic collation by Schäfer and Schubart. But there are
probably more than four letters after *mššann*[*o*, and I discern faint
traces of a letter before -*ṣn* (I see no clear traces of a supraliteral stroke;
cf. Schäfer and Schubart in Abel loc. cit.: "ob -*n*- oder -*n̄*-, lässt sich
nicht sagen"). I remain skeptical about the *a* which Schäfer and Schubart claimed to see (*ka*[·]*sn*), but I can offer nothing convincing in its
place.

16 After *ḍauộ*[G. has a lacuna holding nine letters, but it probably
contained at least twenty.

Below line 16, a rough estimate based on the amount of text presumed missing (part of verse 12 and all of 13) suggests that at least
four lines are lost.

101

Page number: : *rā* : G.; the lower left dot is lost in a lacuna.

1 *aeṭ*- G. Instead of *e* the scribe may have written *o* or *s*; of the
next letter all that remains is the lower tip of a vertical. Very tentatively I propose *aek̠/kane*-, i.e. *āer̄-kane*- "insult": cf. *āēttakatamē* M.
6.12 and *āeiralo* K. 29.12, and see NON V 40 f. For the assimilation
cf. §9.o.

2 *morl̄*[*lo*＼??]*ooukiñña*[?] G. After *morl̄* there is room for only two
letters, of which the first is probably taken by the marker expected between clauses. If rightly read, *morl̄* is the imperfect subjective participle
of *mor*- "be dismissed from," here presumably used in the sense of

"be without" (cf. my note to K. 27.3 in NON VI 130); for the construction cf. §329, and for the absence of a suffix on -*dekel* cf. §295. After
-*kiñña* there is a blank space followed by a lacuna; if a letter had been
written, traces of it would doubtless still be visible.

3 *ǧ[a]u̯ou*- G. in the text, but in his Index he enters *ǧ*[.]*u̯ou*- (126).
After *ǧ* there is a lower tip of a vertical which is not incompatible with *a*;
it is followed by a vertical which projects below the line and suggests
u, *ñ* or (less likely) *r*.

4 *t̠srā*- G., also in Index (120). *t̄ssrā*-, also read by Stricker 444,
is clear on the photograph. Though he keeps G.'s spelling, Zyhlarz
correctly equates the word with K. *tissi* "hassen" (Glossar, 184). The
form is the imperfect predicative participle, as is the following *mallag[r̄(?)]ra*-.

4-5 *mallag[?]ra*- G. (Index, 106: *mallagra*-); note that Hintze has
mallagra- (BanG II 2.4), as does Zyhlarz (§258); but *mallag[r̄]ra*- would
perhaps be a more regular formation; for the morphology cf. *aroua-
gr-e-sô* in WN 10 and see the examples in BanG I 3.1.c.

5 The stroke before *gasknaula* seems misplaced; it appears to belong after the phrase (see above, p. 19).

eïnñgou- G., but what G. read as diaeresis is discoloration.

7 -*non* \\ G., but the second stroke of the clause divider is lost
in a lacuna.

8 *ñadkit̠*[. . . *chris*]*tosin* G.; the lacuna, however, can hardly hold
so many letters. *ñadkigi*[*l chris*]*tosin* suits the available space and
seems to provide acceptable sense; for -*ki*- see §27, and for -*gil(-le)*
as a translation of εἰς cf. 109.12.

8-9 *ou[kour]gille* G., but with *ou[kourra]gille* the restoration is
better suited to the size of the lacuna. For the assimilation cf. §9.r.1
and M. 14.1 *tokder-ra-gl̄-le*.

9-10 *ōnon*[. .]*ñidǧimen*[. . . . .]*n* G. Zyhlarz suggested that *onon*-
"eitel sein" is involved here, and that the passage should be restored
as follows: *onon-[ta] ñid-ǧi-men[-ne-dou̇]n* (a misprint for -*ǧou]n*) = ὅτι
οὐκ εἰς κενὸν ἔδραμον (*Sprachdenkmäler* 191). Zyhlarz has gotten the
general structure, but some refinements in detail are in order: (1) instead of *onon[ta]*, I suggest *ōnona̠[n]*; cf. *tat-an* in the next line and see

§308.c and Anm.; (2) though damaged, *e* appears fairly certain at the end of the line, and since *-lo-/-le-ǧoun* may take the subjunctive (§230), we should restore *nidǧimene[siloǧou]n*, which suits syntax and space (*-leǧou]n* could also be restored, but the latter is not attested with the subjunctive in L.; for the subjunctive with *-loǧoun* see 107.15-16 *ēnerannoǧou[n]*). For *-menesi-* cf. 109.4 *meneri-*.

10-11 *tatan n̩[. .]n̩̄[.]k̩ori̩[.]gǧ[m]s̩selo* G., who writes in a note on *n̄* "or *d.*" But since *n* is not found in word-initial position in Old Nubian, the scribe probably wrote *-non* (i.e. *-lon*: see §264); *-n[o]n* [-] is suited to the space available, and after it I propose *korpaǧi/ms̩selo* as a translation of οὐδὲ . . . ἐκοπίασα; cf. Plumley, *Nubian Literary Text* B 15-16 (Rev 14:13), where *korpaǧǧigoulo* renders ἐκ τῶν κόπων.

11 *oun*: i.e. ὑμῶν; Zyhlarz inadvertently said that this form of the pronoun was "unbelegt" (§99).

piste̩[u . . . . .]a̩lli G. For *piste̩[uei̯-* cf. Plumley, *Nubian Literary Text* B 11 (Rev 14:12) *p̄steuei̯ka* (= τὴν πίστιν) and §29. Before *alli* (the *a* seems certain) I can discern a trace compatible with the upper curve of *ǧ*; for *ǧalli-* cf. 111.1 *ǧallou tiǧkanenigou̩[ka* (= δικαιώματα λατρείας) and Faras 7.1.3 *ǧallatre-*.

12 [.]s̩n̂êus- G. Although the beginning of the line is lost, it seems unlikely than an entire letter is missing. Before *n̂* there survives a curved stroke which could belong to *s*, but *a* is also possible paleographically. The reading *a̩n̂êus-* derives support from an unpublished Qasr Ibrim text, where *enniǧil an̂êu[sigou]ka̩* renders ἄρατε θυσίας (Ps 95[96]:8). For the construction *ǧalli an̂êus-* cf. §295.

12-13 *euarta̩[karr]īl̂ê* [\] [. . . . .] G. With my restoration, ἀλλὰ is translated.

14 *pissrē*: over *e* there is a trace of a stroke not noticed by G.; for the usage cf. 108.13 and see NON VIII 56.

15 [*ketal . . . .*]*tora* G. *tara* is clear on the photograph; it is preceded by the lower part of a vertical which slopes leftward and suggests *l*. Above the preceding lacuna a trema can be seen. Purely hypothetically I suggest *pissanasô on aīda]l̩ tara/[nasô . . .*, "rejoice and

come with me" (+ a word meaning "rejoicing" *aut sim.*?), an adaptation of χαίρετε καὶ συγχαίρετέ μοι.

Below *tara* there is a trace (not reported by G.), apparently of the line separating lessons (cf. 106.3; 112.2, 5; 115.4); below that we have the beginning of the next lesson (for the restoration cf. 112.3, and for the Ammonian number see Schäfer-Schmidt, *Handschriften* 603). Here the Greek has ὑμεῖς ἐστε τὸ ἅλας τῆς γῆς · ἐὰν δὲ τὸ ἅλας μωρανθῇ, ἐν τίνι ἁλισθήσεται; Since what we have of the Nubian version of these words (see 102.1) does not readily correspond with the Greek, we are likely to be dealing with paraphrase rather than with translation. Considerations of space suggest that no more than two lines have been lost at the bottom of the page. G. notes at the end of his transcript of this page: "[Several lines lost.]"

17 Of this line (not in G.) the last letter may be *n*, and perhaps we should restore *ourou ei]n̥/[no*, i.e. ὑμεῖς ἐστε (cf. §§161 and 296).

102

1 For the beginning of this section see 101.15n.

ṭikkennan. G. but the clause marker is clear. In *Sprachdenkmäler* 194, Zyhlarz was presumably misled by G.'s transcript and proposed]-*tik-ken-nan*[.], which he translated as "mag man [scil. salzen]." This form he regarded as "Thematischer Adverbialis," together with *moudoutakkennana* in WN 5. But the latter's morphology is not at all obvious, and it is perhaps preferable to take *ṭikkennan* as a "Collative" (cf. §180 and note especially *kelknnan* "wie sie sind" in M. 16.3 as well as *ṭkknno* "wie gegeben" in St. 13.2-3); if this interpretation of *ṭikkennan* is correct, it is probably an addition of the translator: "as they are wont to give"; cf. 100.10-11n., 101.15n.

ouēraṅi-: for the stroke see NON VIII 56 n. 5.

2 *odñoōsa ǧirkera*: see BanG III 6.2.2.

4 *pikit*[ ] G.; *pikit[a̧]*- is suggested by Zyhlarz (§§280.b.1, 296.a), perhaps rightly. Though we might expect **kosmosina pikita*- (see BanG II 2.6), the evidence of M. 9.16-10.1 (*kuriāken oukour' einnon*) shows that the genitive in -*n* may be construed with a regens in the predicative.

6-7 _ātm̄i̱_[.]_rose̱_[. .] G., for which Zyhlarz proposed _ātm̄g[i]rose[n]_ "wenn man bereits anzündet" (Text I S.37 n. 2); he may be right, but the _g_ should be dotted. After the lacuna the letter may be _a_ or _l_.

7 _telo le_[G., but there is no word division in the manuscript and the articulation is not clear. _telo-_ may be related to K. _têl_, D. _telê_ "glühen, sehr heiss sein" (Massenbach 234).

maš[ ] G.; _maš[en]_ follows Zyhlarz (§213). The word is presumably to be associated with Sahidic Coptic _maše_ (see G., Index 106).

8 _tauȏ_[. . . .]_a̱o̱_[G.; _tauȏ_ is followed by a lacuna sufficient for two letters, next there is a trace of a vertical stroke, and then comes a lacuna that can hold one letter. After the lacuna, _a_ and _o_ seem inevitable as readings. For _tauȏlo_ cf. St. 12.7-8.

8-9 G. read _kera[lo_ in line 8, but consideration of the space available suggests that -_lo_, especially if it is followed by a clause marker (as in line 2), belongs to the beginning of line 9.

9 [. . . . .]_o̱nnôa̱_ G., who adds in a note: "Apparently final 'that it may shine'." For the construction see §184; the lacuna may have held the emphatic particle -_a_, for which see §275.b and c. The drift of the Nubian seems to be as follows: " . . . he should not place it under a measure but should place it so that it be on a lamp-
[-]
stand . . . " (i.e. [—_dô pik_]_onnoa̱_[(_ā_)] (cf. K. 19.10, 30.15) [—_keralo enkô_ ⟍).

103

Page number: G. prints : _rg_ :, but the stroke over the letters is visible, and the lower left dot is lost in the lacuna.

2-3 See Stricker 441 n. 4: " 'a jot (I) or one in the _pisti_ which is on it'. Here _pisti_, modern _fissi_ or 'sprinkling', means the two points written over the jot (Ï)." Cf. also G. ad loc.

4 _ṅokadena_ ⟍ G., but the manuscript has only one stroke, in black; i.e. only the left part of the clause marker was written (see above, p. 19).

5-6 _eṉ s̄[s]ana_: the restoration is due to Zyhlarz (§110); G. has _eṉs̄_[.]_ana_; for the construction see next note.

7 *kouṣ[sa .]ạ* G., also in the Index, 104; on p. 85 he prints *kous[sar]l̄*, a future participle. The latter Zyhlarz takes over in his discussion of the participle of Future I (§149). In BanG I 4, Hintze suggests that the form should be *-arril* (cf. BanG V 2.2.b). I propose *kous[l̄goul]l* and for the construction I refer to Plumley, *Nubian Literary Text* A 16-20 (Rev 14:9-10) *en̄ essana ṅarmitn̄ eigonka doukl̄goul tan taṅsn̄ edkon ten koñn̄ tn̄nattddô ettolgoul · on ten eiōnon eldo · tallo ṅerra . . .*, "those—whoever these are—who worship the image of the beast and have received the sign of his name on their forehead and on their right hand, he will drink . . ." (εἴ τις προσκυνεῖ τὸ θηρίον καὶ τὴν εἰκόνα αὐτοῦ καὶ λαμβάνει χάραγμα ἐπὶ τοῦ μετώπου αὐτοῦ ἢ ἐπὶ τὴν χεῖρα αὐτοῦ, καὶ αὐτὸς πίεται . . .). For the shift from (generic) plural to singular see NON IV and below, 115.12n. Unless the writing is cramped, there is hardly room for *kous[sl̄goul]l*, despite the double *s* in *kss̄itaken* (K. 29.14-15) and M. K. *kusse* "loosen" (see G., Index 104); cf. 107.14n.

[-]
7-8 *eigouk ẹ[ko]ul[li]ğa* G., who writes in his note ad loc.: "Perhaps for *eik koulliğa* 'teach them this.' " The trace after *eigouk* could be *e*, but *a* is also a permissible interpretation, and the following lacuna can probably hold only one letter. I suggest *eigoukạ [o]ul[li]ğa* "teaching men," a reading which avoids assumption of scribal error and is better suited to the space available (for *-ạ [o]u-* cf. especially *-aou-* in *dalla ouel-* above in line 3). For the word *oull(i)* "teach," I refer to the noun *oullakke* which translates διδάσκαλος in two unpublished texts from Qasr Ibrim (Jn 11:28 and 13:14); note also K. 26.2-3 *eitei êkkoulll̄-dal* "with a teacher" (*êkk-* = "instruct"; cf. St. 19.8-9, where *ekk-īt-* probably renders παιδαγωγός, just as *r̄kdesō* corresponds to νομο-θέτησον in NI 78/51 i 18 [Ps 26(27):11]). Note that with this revision in reading, οὕτως is not translated, but the word is omitted in part of the Greek tradition (see the apparatus to the Greek text).

8 *toukḷ[. . . . .]e[. . . . .]ô* G. After *touk-*, *l*, *a* or *m* is possible. A letter, apparently *a* or *l*, is visible before the final *ô*.

9 Traces remain of this line, but they are not reported by G.

10 Of this line, not reproduced by G., a final *u* is visible.

104

Page number: : r̄d : G.

1 [.]ellô: this corresponds either to πώρωσις (cf. BanG IV 2) or to ἀπὸ μέρους; if the latter (so G.), then perhaps the scribe wrote min/-del-lô: cf. mindi mn̄dilo for κατὰ μέρος in 112.1.

1-2 doullaṅ/[ar]asin G., but doullaṅ[a]/[r]asin conforms to the pattern of word division regular in L. (see above, p. 20), and the beginning of line 2 seems slightly better suited to [r] than to [ar]; there is also room for a at the end of line 1. -sin here translates ὅτι; cf. 112.2.

3 [t]ọra: cf. M. 10.7 tora kisna; [t]ạra (cf. 113.3) is less likely as a reading.

4 [g]ralo G. For ḡr- see on NI 78/26 i 9, STB 2 (1980) 25.

4-5 ṅarta[k]kona G. Although the sheet breaks off after ṅarta, and there is room for another letter, I see no reason to introduce an unusual spelling: ṅartakona is the expected form (see §158.1.a).

6 gp̄r-: though damaged, the stroke probably once extended to the r, as in K. 29.14 (see NON VIII 57).

7 teni[ā] ṭilliḳiṅkaneka G.

7-8 iak[ô]/b[. . . . .]ketal G., but there is no trace of b at the beginning of line 8. For my restoration īāk̦ọ[biō (i.e. īākôbi-lo: §201)
cf. §202 and note especially 105.12-13 diạriô tak[k]a auoulōs- "to save him from death." For on]ketal "and" see St. 29.3 onketal (o, though damaged, is certain, and Zyhlarz's [ē]nketal, Text III S.82, cannot be read) and a Qasr Ibrim text cited in Jakobielski, Inscriptions 151 n. 3: onketal; it is restored in 107.19. In §315.c Zyhlarz suggested tek]-ketal "sie betreffend," but for this I have no parallel, and it hardly matches the Greek.

8-9 digiṛ[t/ G.; the form most likely ends in -ti, as Zyhlarz noted (§153 Anm.; cf. also §26), and a trace of ink not incompatible with t is discernible at the beginning of line 9. With the personal pronoun an we would expect digiṛṭ[il (or -ṭ[l): see Stricker 444; and for the subjective instead of the predicative cf. 109.6 eñna salssin eñnasñ ālel and K. 31.10-11 tan ğannon eñno.

9 [. . . . . .]*llen.* G. The right stroke of the clause marker survives, but it is written very close to the left stroke. The text probably translates αὐτοῖς, but its restoration is not obvious.

[-]

10 *ostr[a]ǧeri-* G., to which Hintze objects on the grounds that the formation is anomalous (BanG III 6.2.3); he notes: "man könnte hier . . . *osi-ǧra* vermuten und statt *-ǧ(eri)* ist wohl besser *-deri* (l. sg. fut.) zu lesen." In BanG V 3.1.2 he offers another reading: *os-tir[a]-deri.* Neither of Hintze's suggestions is paleographically possible, and

[-]

I propose *os[i]gạ[ǧ]ǧeri-*, which squares with the traces and seems formally unobjectionable. For *-gaǧǧ-*, i.e. *-gar- + -ǧ-* see BanG III 6.2.1 and cf. NI 78/5 b ii 2 *tṃmigaǧǧa.* For the causative cf. e.g. M. 12.15-16 *ōōkr̄sna.*

11 *-de*: here the Greek has μέν; *-de* is balanced by *-eion* in the next line (cf. 110.2 and note).

12 *-gr[ā]eion*: the stroke above *a* is visible.

13 [*tll̄n*] G.

14 *ṭitti[goulde . . . . dekel . .*] G.

15 *ouọ*[G. The doubtful *o* could also be *r*; if it is, we have the beginning of verse 30 (ὥσπερ γὰρ ὑμεῖς . . .).

Below line 15 the text probably continued to the end of verse 31 (see Schäfer-Schmidt, *Handschriften* 603). A rough estimation, as well as comparison with the end of 105 (see 105.17n.), suggests that at least three additional lines are required for this amount of text. If the page also held a Gospel entry, as Schäfer and Schmidt suggest (loc. cit.), it will have had to be quite short: probably no more than a single line containing the date, name of the Gospel in question, and the Ammonian number; there is not likely to be room for the incipit and explicit as in 112.3-5.

105

1 *apos*: *t* is clearly visible, though damaged; it is absent in G.'s transcript as well as in that of Schäfer-Schmidt, *Handschriften* 604.

3 *oktakol-*: this implies ὁ καλούμενος (see the apparatus to the Greek); cf. below, line 6, where *pesol* renders ὁ λαλήσας.

3-4 *arônnānon* G.

4 *eikarigralo* G.

5 *archīereōs-* G.; the correct spelling (but without diaeresis) appears in the Index (88).

5-6 *eīniā menona*: for the syntax see my comments in NON VII 137 n. 11.

6-7 *ei[r]ou* G.; the appositive ending suggests that the pronoun goes with what follows (cf. §296.a); the Greek was therefore probably misarticulated: υἱός μου εῖ, σὺ ἐγὼ σήμερον γεγέννηκά σε.

7 *ōn* appears to connect the two clauses. For its postponement cf. M. 4.8; K 21.7; St. 6.7.

8 *kell[ô]* \ G.

9 *keta[lle]n̥[.]*: though there is room for a final letter, and *keta[lle]n̥[l̄]* is a possibility, the word may be complete as it stands: see 106.17n.

11 *[s̄]sn̄*: I can discern a faint trace of the stroke over the initial *s*. [. . . . .]l̥ G.

12 *s̄kelittil* G. (correctly reproduced in the Index, 97).

diā̱r̥iô G. The stroke expected over *ô* cannot be read (see NON VIII 55).

14 *[de . . . . .]e̥-* G. After the lacuna *l* is also possible and perhaps preferable on morphological grounds (cf. BanG IV 5.3.1).

15 [. . . . .] *ueleg̑oun* G. After a lacuna of ± 6 letters there is a supraliteral stroke followed by what is perhaps *n*. The first part of the line may have contained a translation of προσενέγκας: [± 5 *-l̄*]; the remainder will then have rendered ἀπὸ τῆς εὐλαβείας (cf. §230).

16] *enl̥l̄[* G., but the line clearly ends after the second *l*. (Note that here and in the next line, G. does not indicate the approximate number of letters presumed missing in the initial lacunae.) The word doubtless corresponds to ὧν, with the second *l* marking an appositive to the subject: "the one who is the Son." The preceding *a* (not reported

by G.) suggests *tot*]*a* (υἱός); before this probably stood a translation of εἰσακουσθείς.

17] *t̆ğt*[G., but again, the word ends the line. What G. read as a doubtful *t* may be a supraliteral stroke; it is followed by a letter which suggests *ğ*, but the absence of a stroke over the following *t* is surprising, and perhaps what resembles *ğ* is in fact scribal correction, e.g. *o* with a suprascript letter (cf. 100.1). We may have here a rendition of τὴν ὑπακοήν, though its formation is not clear; a translation of ἀφ' ὧν ἔπαθεν may have preceded.

Below line 17 G. writes: "[One (?) line lost.]" But a hypothetical reconstruction of the Old Nubian suggests that at least three lines are missing. Line 18 could render ἔμαθεν (for τὴν ὑπακοήν see preceding paragraph) ... καὶ τελειωθείς; 19 and 20 could correspond to πᾶσιν τοῖς ὑπακούουσιν αὐτῷ ... σωτηρίας αἰωνίου (for ἐγένετο ... αἴτιος see 106.1).

106

1 [.]*na* G.

1-2 *ar*[*ch*]*êiēreōs-* G.; *s* is corrected or remade.

3 At the beginning of the line G. prints [. .], but the space seems better suited to one letter of normal size. In §233, Zyhlarz tentatively

?

suggested [*tr*]*e-*, but the space appears somewhat too narrow for this otherwise unparalleled formation.

4 Before *eп̄п̄ka* G. prints [:], but the lower dot of the colon is visible.

eп̄п̄ka: i.e. *eп̄ka*; cf. below, line 8.

5 *pesiğerī*: see NON IX 62-64.

aīā[?] G., but though there is space for one letter, none is required. In §340, Zyhlarz inadvertently printed *aīka* in citing this passage. For *aīā* cf. §11 and see also 109.15.

6 *konkoālô*: an athematic finalis, for which cf. §340 and see NI 78/5 c i 10]*tormenkoā*. Since an athematic formation appears in a subordinate clause when the latter's subject is identical with that of the

main clause (§332), the Nubian translator probably understood the Greek as follows: Ἵνα ἐν ἐμοὶ εἰρήνην ἔχητε, ἐν τῷ κόσμῳ θλῖψιν ἔχετε.

6-7 ma̰kīka G. The sheet breaks off after ma- (in which the a, though damaged, seems certain), and there is easily room for another letter. I propose ma[ī]/kīka, and for a parallel I refer to an unpublished Qasr Ibrim text, where maïk[ī- translates θλῖψις in 2 Cor 1:4. Similarly, we should probably read maịktou for G.'s ma///ktou in gr. 2.9 (an maịktou ǧm̄mīlo = ἐκ πασῶν τῶν θλίψεών μου Ps 33[34]:5). The word is a noun formation (cf. §26), and the verb on which it is based, maïk-, can easily mean "afflict" in both its occurrences in the corpus (hitherto it was hypothetically taken to mean "shame": see Griffith 106 and Zyhlarz, Glossar 179): M. 2.4 maïkarisna "she was afflicted" (see BanG III 6.1.2 for the formation) and St. 8.10-11 maiken salagouē- "words of afflic-tion."

8 ai G.

kos[mos]k G.

-sn̄: perhaps causal (cf. §278); it may imply γάρ in the Greek Vorlage (see the apparatus).

8-9 pes̰[i]ǧ[. . . .]eịon G. After ǧ there are traces which suggest ar (cf. especially -ar- in pooggara, line 10). I propose pes̰[i]ǧar[alo]eịon, which suits the size of the lacuna and provides acceptable sense. If rightly restored, the construction exemplifies the use of the predicative participle, with or without -lo, as the main verb: see §§187, 316, BanG I 3.1.c and NON VII. For the position of the participle I refer to an unpublished Qasr Ibrim text which contains a slightly free rendering of Jn 13:16 (οὐδὲ ἀπόστολος μείζων τοῦ πέμψαντος αὐτόν): eitr̄takara tak eitrolọ̄ (i.e. eitrol-lô) gôeia dauel̄ ende "nor was there sent one greater than the one who sent him."

9-10 tr[ika G.

10 harmi]l̰āgille G.; this is possible, but a stroke over a is unusual in this position (see NON VIII 55 f.). The space seems too short for harm]ị̄ā-, and I propose harm]l̰ā-; cf. above, 103.1 harmnā, and NON VIII loc. cit.

pessna̰ G.

[—]   ?

11 *ṭṣ̌atī-* G.; Zyhlarz's *tihati-* (Glossar, 184) cannot be read. For *taraṭ-* cf. K. 28.1-2 *tarat-* (ὥρα: see NON VI No. 5) and Plumley, *Nubian Literary Text* A 6 *tarat-* (ὥρα: Rev 14:7).

12 *tre[sô* G.

13-14 *tš̄?]sin-* G. For the common assimilation of *r + s* to *ss* see §9.q. Also possible is *ṭ[r]sin-*, as in M. 7.6 *tr̄sna.*

15 *[ke]tallenka* G.

At the end of the line G. prints .╲; in reality, only a trace remains of the first stroke, and the second is gone completely.

16 *[ti]ǧ̆ǧ̆[iknoua]* ╲ G.; for the revision in reading see NON I.

16-17 *eñ[na]na* G., but though the line breaks off after *eñ*, the lacuna seems too narrow for *[na]*, and only *eñna* (ἐστιν) is required (see next note).

17 *na* . . . . *len̠* ╲ G. My restoration is purely hypothetical; it is based upon *añǧi ellen ḳetallenka* in line 15. Here I assume that *keta]l̠len* stands for **ketallen-l̄* (for the use of *-l̄* cf. 109.6 *eñna salśsin eñnasn̄ ālel*; for the phonetic changes, *n + l → nn* and *nn → n* see §§9.c and 10 and cf. *-deken* for **-dekel-n̄* and *-dekel* for **-dekel-l̄*: see NON II 252 f.).

18 . . . . *eiāri* G. For *eiāri* see NON X; it is apparently a present infinitive in apposition to the subject; i.e. "this is the eternal life, to know you . . . "

After *eiāri* the scribe reverses the color sequence usually used for the clause marker and places the red stroke before the black (see above, p. 19).

18-19 *e[ ]/[* . . . . *chris]tosika* G. My restoration, again, is exempli gratia; cf. 109.7 and for the syntax see Abel 51.

[-]

20 . . . .] *sktīdô* G. What I hypothetically restore suits the space available; for its components cf. above, lines 13-14 and 108.2-3 *aîon [ei]dgillesn̄ kiresn̄.*

ñe[eil] G.; see next note.

21 . . . . ⁻]*k[* . . .]*gr̠[* . . . G. Possibly we should restore as follows: *ñe[eik]/[auā ein aîka diss]ñ̠k[(a)*, "doing the thing which

you gave me" (τὸ ἔργον τελειώσας ὃ δέδωκάς μοι); for *ṅeeik* equivalent
to *ṅeeik-k(a)* cf. BanG IV 5.4 and M. 13.9 (*ṅak* = *ṅak-k*), and for
the construction as a whole cf. 110.9-10 and also perhaps M. 8.16-9.4
eṅka ankimṅnai eĩtou oⱥenna ekka denǧska · ṅ̄ssou mênan k̄ssela iǧǧanasa,
"erinnerst Du Dich nicht mehr daran, dass es uns eine Frau gegeben
hat, damit wir es in der Kirche des heiligen Menas abgeben?" (Zyhlarz,
Text I S.33; for discussion of *denǧska* see BanG I 4.5); the Menas passage suggests that . .] . *gṛ*[±2] may have represented a similar construction: . .] . *gṛ*[*e/sa* or . .] . *gṛ*[*eā* (cf. 109.1, 112.10, and see §181). Of
the doubtful *n* after the lacuna (*diss*]*n̄*-), part of the second vertical remains.

107

1 *elon* G., but I can discern part of a stroke over the first letter.
ṅokou: resumed by *ṅokou* in the next line and probably not a mistake, despite Hintze's reservations (BanG I 4.2).
dinesô ＼: the clause marker seems misplaced; logically it belongs
after *eriō̄rô* in the next line (see above, p. 19).
2 *eiriôōrô* G. (correct in Index, 110).
3 *eiriōtǧô* G. (*eiriotǧô* in Index, 122).
doun koussika: I follow Abel's interpretation (44); he takes *doun*
as an adverbialis and translates the phrase "den ich hatte, als ich bei
dir war." This seems preferable to Zyhlarz's articulation, *doun-kous-s-i*
"ich hatte besessen" (§168), since the verb *doun-* "besitzen" is not elsewhere attested in the extant material.
4-5 *eigouka . . . denǧisingoul*: probably the translator thus articu-
lated the Greek: . . . τοῖς ἀνθρώποις · οὓς ἔδωκας . . . σοὶ ἦσαν. Cf.
Hintze, BanG IV 1.
5 *ǧool*: this could mean "when I came" (cf. M. 3.12-13 *koumpoun
kakī ouekka*, for which see BanG IV 5.1 and Stricker 452), but "when
they came" seems more likely: cf. §329 and NI 78/26 ii 18 (Jude 15),
where *mesī* translates ἁμαρτωλοί (see my note ad loc. in *STB* 2 [1980] 31).
For a similar interpretation of the Greek (οὓς ἔδωκάς μοι ἐκ τοῦ κόσμου)
I refer to one of the manuscripts cited in Horner's apparatus to the

Sahidic New Testament: *aiouenh̄ pekran ebol n̄n̄rôme n̄taktaau nai nebol hm̄ pkosmos.*

6 *-gouēlo* \ G., but the red stroke is missing (see above, p. 19).

8 *m[s̱]š[a]ṇka* G.

9 *kellôka tekka tiğğesiḳ[a*: G. translates "The like thou gavest unto them" (see note ad loc.); this implies *tiğğesiṇ[ka*, paleographically less attractive than *tiğğesik[a*, which corresponds to δέδωκα. Probably haplography occasioned the reading in the Old Nubian: πάντα ὅσα δέδω- κάς μοι ⟨παρὰ σοῦ εἰσίν· ὅτι τὰ ῥήματα ἃ ἔδωκάς [or the variant δέδωκας: see NA^{app}] μοι⟩ δέδωκα αὐτοῖς. *kellôka* = "all"; see Stri- cker 452 and NON III; cf. also Abel 36, who translates the passage "sie erkannten, dass ich alles, was du mir gabst, ihnen gegeben habe."

10 *aï*] G.; the expected *an* appears in Abel 36; cf. also Stricker 453.

11 After *krēsika* the clause marker has the red stroke before the black, contrary to usual practice (see above, p. 19).

13-14 *ğouria-* G. (correctly reproduced in Index, 126).

14 *sen[im]n̄ṇeso* G., who writes in his note ad loc.: "Or *-lo.*" The latter appears slightly better paleographically: cf. the *l* in *pala* in line 11 (for the particle cf. §204.c). The space is not adequate for *sen[nim]n̄-* (or *sen[nm̄]n̄-*) mentioned in BanG III 3.2.2.; cf. 103.7n. Cf. *tok-* . . . *tokk-* M. 9.7 and 9.

15 *-[go]un* G.

15-16 *ğ[ouriā* . . . . *e]n̄ēnerannoğou[n lenkô*] \ [. . . . .] G. But there is no trace of the clause marker, and we hardly have room for more than six letters of normal size after *lenkô* \, scarcely adequate for a translation of τὰ ἐμὰ πάντα. I have preferred to place *-enkô* \ after *ğ[ouriā* (or *-lenkô* without clause marker) and thereby to leave ample room in line 16 for the Nubian equivalent of τὰ ἐμὰ πάντα. For the latter I suggest, exempli gratia, *annagoul kellô*; cf. Ben. 2, 4, 20, 24, and see NON III. Another possible restoration is *anna mššangoul.*

17 *eñnam[ê* . . . .] G.; *anna-*] is Zyhlarz's suggestion: see §319.

18-19 *ter̤[* . . . .]ṇo[. . . .]*en[* . . . . . *kos*] G. The dotted let- ters all seem certain, and the first and third lacunae hold more than G. indicated. In line 19 it is hard not to think of *ṇo[kka d]en[-*; i.e. the

Greek was ἐδόξασάς με. *aīka* probably preceded, at the end of 18, and *teṛ*[is the beginning of the rendition of καὶ ... ἐν αὐτοῖς; the obvious *teṛ*[*iāeion* makes the line too short, and so I suggest *teṛ*[*iōg̃ōāeion*; note that *tadiog̃ōā* renders ἐν αὐτῇ in NI 78/35 i 27 (Ps 86[87]: 5), and *eidiōg̃ōa* corresponds to ἐν σοί in ii 8 of the same text (Ps 86:7); cf. also gr. 10.1 *tan̄ṣṣllog̃ōā*. *d*]*en*[- I have restored as *d*]*en*[*isnā*, but *d*]*en*[*aralê* would also be possible (cf. line 6 above). The lacuna following is the right size for *onketal kos*]- (continued on the next page); for *onketal* see 104.7-8n.

108

1 -*la* G.

doumminelô G.; thus reproduced by Zyhlarz §10 as an instance of simplification of doubled consonants. The form is given correctly in G.'s Index (93, s.v. *dou-*).

4 Note that the Old Nubian omits a translation of ᾧ δέδωκάς μοι after *tan̄slōkô* (not indicated in G.'s edition).

5 *ouērinī*: see NON VIII 56 n. 5.

doukoannoā G., and so quoted by Zyhlarz §236; it is correctly reproduced in G.'s Index (93) and also by Zyhlarz in §184.

6 -*la* G.

I follow G. in restoring *an* at the end of the line; with it, however, the line is perhaps somewhat too long, and it may not have been written.

7 *dou*ẹ[*n t*]*auklō-* G.; though damaged, the *e* seems relatively certain, and *doun*[(cf. 107.3) cannot be read. There are other possibil-
[-]
ities for restoration: e.g. *dou*ẹ[*si* or *dou*ṣ[*si*, preterite subjunctives of *dou-* and *doul-*, respectively (for the assimilation, *l* + *s* → *ss*, not listed in Zyhlarz, cf. 109.6 *salssin* and K. 30.16 *nodssn̄*).

7-8 *ei*[*d*]*ñig̃*[*ar*]*ra*: I follow G.'s restoration; he dotted all the visible letters except *ei* and the final *a*, but the reading seems inevitable. The lacuna is too large for -*g̃*[*a*]*ra*, a perfect predicative participle, which would approximate the tense of the Greek (ἐτήρουν). If -*g̃*[*ar*]*ra* is correct (and the space suits it), either it is an alternative spelling for -*g̃ara* (cf. §10 and note that in Plumley, *Nubian Literary Text* B 24

[Rev 14:14] *darra* seems to equal **da-ara*), or else the Future I predicative participle is here used to mean "I would save them."

9 *de[nǵsnk e]idñiǧise* G. (cf. 110.7), but the lacuna can hold no more than five letters. I tentatively suggest *de[ssin*; for the subjunctive see 111.5-6 *douēsan*, 114.11-13n. and Abel 51, and for the assimilation (from *den-sin*) cf. especially 110.9-10 *dissi̧n-*, also 107.3 and 112.2. G.'s restoration translates οὓς δέδωκας; the revision, if correct, shows that the Greek model was ᾧ δέδωκας. The punctuation in the manuscript suggests that the Greek was interpreted thus: . . . ἐτήρουν αὐτούς · ἐν τῷ ὀνόματί σου ᾧ δέδωκάς μοι ἐφύλαξα . . .

10 *dappimennalô* \: the red stroke is omitted (see above, p. 19). G.'s transcript replaces the stroke with a punctum.

11 *totlenkô*: — G.

12 For the clause marker, the scribe has reversed the normal color sequence and has placed red before black (see above, p. 19).

einn̄ka[eion] G.

13 *pesiǧrē*: for the stroke see NON VIII 56.

14 *te[rio]ǵ[oṵn] ko̧ann[o]ā* G., but *ko̧ann[o]ā* is not a complete formation: it lacks the verb. I suggest *tȩr[iā] ko̧nko̧anno̧ā*, "in order that they may have in themselves" (ἵνα ἔχωσιν . . . ἐν ἑαυτοῖς). · For *teriā* cf. M. 3.1 *tariā pessna*. The stroke over *a* (which G. took as *ǧ*) resembles that in *ōken* 112.4. The *r* in *tȩr[iā]* and the *k* in *ko̧n-* are extremely faint; the following *-o̧n* is more secure as a reading.[1]

At the end of the line G. reads: —

15 *ein* G., but *en̄* seems slightly better suited to the size of the lacuna.

At the end of the line G. reads *t]iǧǧis̩i̧ ou[*, but there is no word division. The sheet breaks off after *-ou*, and there is room for another letter. Possibly a particle, elsewhere unattested, is involved, of which the first two letters are *ou*; if so, the Nubian might have been designed to mean "since I gave them your word . . . " Cf. Abel 37.

---

[1] In a discussion of this passage in my paper, "Griffith's Old Nubian Lectionary," *Proceedings of the First Nilo-Saharan Linguistics Colloquium* (Leiden 1981) 148, I gave the revision as *te[riā kon]ko̧ann[o̧]ā*. Made prior to autoptic examination of the manuscript, this revision is subject to the modifications set forth above.

16 . . . .]*monğ*[. . . G. My restoration is exempli gratia. Doubtless *kosmosī* stood in the lacuna, but its exact position I cannot ascertain.

Below line 16, Ġ. writes "[Two (?) lines lost.]" The text, as a hypothetical reconstruction suggests, is better suited to three lines:

> [*kosmosilo ğôāra menerannoğoun* ⟍]
> [*anna kosmosilo ğôāra meneri*]
> [*kellô* ⟍ *kosmosilo tekka* 4-8]   15

"because they have not come from the world, just as I have not come from the world. (15) (And I do not ask that you take [see 109.1]) them from the world . . . " (ὅτι οὐκ εἰσὶν ἐκ τοῦ κόσμου καθὼς ἐγὼ οὐκ εἰμὶ ἐκ τοῦ κόσμου. (15) οὐκ ἐρωτῶ ἵνα ἄρῃς αὐτοὺς ἐκ τοῦ κόσμου . . .). For the reconstruction cf. 107.15-16, 109.2-4. In 109.1 *ōs-* is probably the end of a compound (cf. Zyhlarz, Text I S.37 n. 2), e.g. *auoul-*]/*ōs-* (cf. 105.13; for the word division see 114.11-12).

109

1 *-eiōn* G., but over *o* there is surface discoloration, not ink.

2 *-lō*: *lā* G. The photograph which he used (see his Tafel I) has a dark spot on the lower right of the *o*; it is not ink, but it makes the *o* resemble *a*. Before *-lō* the vertical of the *t* is lost through abrasion.

3-4 *gôāra*: possibly the translator derived εἰσίν . . . εἰμί from εἰμι and not from εἰμί.

3 *minnelô*: *l* is corrected or remade. *minnana-* is expected: cf. BanG I 2.2.3 n. 9.

5 *ālel*: there is a point of ink over *l*. It is absent in G.'s transcription and may be accidental.

6 *salssin*: i.e. *sal-* + *-l-* (subjective marker) + *-sin*; for the assimilation see on 108.7. *-sin* is perhaps causal: see on 106.8.

ālel: the clause marker placed before this word seems to belong after it (see above, p. 19). G. omits the stroke over *a* (also in his Index, 87).

7 *-lagil* G. (the stroke over *a* is also omitted in the Index, 90).

8 -*lagia* G.; it is spelled correctly, though without the stroke over the *a*, in the Index, 90. In §321 Zyhlarz gives the word as -*lagī*.

As regards the clause marker in this line, G. prints it in full, but the right stroke is lost in a lacuna.

n̄ssan̄resô G.; for the stroke, lost in a lacuna above *e*, cf. 108.13 and n. -*n̄re*-: for -*gre*-? (cf. above, line 5).

10 *n̄ssan̄areinī*: see BanG III 4.1.

10-11 [*doukk*]*oan̄noā* G.

11 *a*[*o*]*u̯out*- G.

-*ǧour*[*iā*] G.; the stroke over *a* is visible, and very faint traces of *a* remain.

12 In the clause marker after -*m̯*[*i*]*n̯nelo* (*m̯*[*in*]*nelo* G.) both strokes are black (see above, p. 19).

aigil G.

14 -*en*[*kô* \\] G.

ouērinī: see 108.5n.

15 *ēr*[. . . . .]*iā* G. Before *iā* I discern traces not incompatible with *a*. G.'s *ēr̯* is likely; a faint trace follows, too ambiguous for identification. As an exempli-gratia restoration I propose *ēr̯o*[*u papo en̄na*] *a̯iā*, "you, father, are in me" (σύ, πάτερ, ἐν ἐμοὶ . . .). For the construction, *ēr-ou* + vocative, cf. St. 8.3-5 *ourou an en̄n̄aegouēke*.

16 *e*[. . . . .]*tek* G. My hypothetical restoration suits the size of the lacuna; for the syntax cf. 108.5-6.

17 [. . . .]*eir*[. . . . .]*ti* G. (i.e. *ti*]/[*ǧ*]*ǧise*: see my note to 110.1). For [*ketal*], which fits the space, cf. above, 9-10. Presumably *eir*- stands for *er*- (cf. St. 2.7 and 30.8-9 *en̄nou*), and *e*{*i*} *ri*[*ā* should be restored; if the scribe actually intended *eiriā*, the meaning will be "in you." The rest of the line I have filled out exempli gratia. At the end there is a trace of ink, not incompatible with *l* (it was not reported by G.).

G. evidently assumed that no lines were missing at the bottom of the page, but a hypothetical translation of the corresponding Greek seems to require two additional lines below 17:

[*p̄steueikonnoā* (\\) *ein aīk eitreska* \\ *aī*]   22
[*on n̄okou ein aīka dissinka tekka tiǧ*]/*ǧise* (110.1)

" . . . in order that the world may believe that you sent me. (22) And I gave to them the glory which you gave to me" (ἵνα ὁ κόσμος πιστεύῃ ὅτι σύ με ἀπέστειλας. (22) κἀγὼ τὴν δόξαν ἣν δέδωκάς μοι δέδωκα αὐτοῖς). Cf. 107.12, 110.5 (and n.), 9-10. The clause marker before *ein* in line 18 seems optional: cf. 107.12 and 110.5.

110

Page number: : r[ī :] G.

1 *ti/ǧ]ǧise* G., but the word division is unusual. There is a small lacuna before *-ǧise*, but it may have been filled with the upper left curve of *ǧ*.

2 *-[n]a* G.

eidde̢ [*aila aide*] G., for which the space does not appear to suffice. For *aīā* cf. 106.5, 109.15. *aīon* may be preferable to *aīde*: cf. 104.11n., and also K. 32.7-9 *-de . . . -on*.

3-4 *ouereinnik̢[iriṅilg]/ou̢l* G. But several objections may be raised: (1) the word division between lines is surprising; (2) the *o* which G. prints at the beginning of line 4 belongs in the lacuna: it is restored, not read; (3) in view of the Greek, τετελειωμένοι, we might expect a perfect participle, not the imperfect which G. restores (cf. St. 19.6, where *teuolgoun* renders πεπλανημένων [see Zyhlarz, Text III S. 34 n. 1]); (4) the overall construction is not clear; in particular, the plural subject with its verb in the singular is without parallel (the pattern exemplified in 115.12—see note ad loc.—is not analogous). To obviate these difficulties, I tentatively suggest *eṅni ouereinni̢l* [*kiriṅarei*]/[*n*]*i̢l doukkonnoā*, literally "in order that what pertains to these people's being one may be fulfilled." [*kiriṅarei*]/[*n*]*i̢l*, which suits the available space, follows the pattern of 109.10 *ṅssaṅareinl̄* (see note ad loc.). *ouereinni̢l* is a nisbe formation, comparable to St. 2.6-7, where a series of nouns culminates in *-de[k]ennī* (see §222); Ben. 8 *auwasin ǧounil* "that which belongs to the rain-shower's going" (?) (see NON II 253 and n. 3); WN 4 *ōnonkaeigounl̄* (cf. Zyhlarz, *Sprachdenkmäler* 192 f.).

4-5 *kosmo̢si̢l* [*iakkon*]*noā* G. The space seems insufficient for this restoration; G. appears to have attempted to reduce its length by reading *iak-* instead of *eiak-*, the spelling when the verb is securely read. Before the lacuna, I can discern a faint speck suggesting the lower left of *a*, and I therefore read *a̤[kkon]noā*, i.e. *ar-konnoā*; for the verb see below, note to 12-13.

5 *eitreka*: presumably a mistake for *eitreska*, the form in 107.12. If the form were correct here, we would expect **eitrēka* (cf. *eitrēsin-* 109.7 and see NON VIII 56). If *eitreka* is right, and the stroke is simply omitted, it is a present infinitive. Cf. BanG I 4.5 and Abel 38.

6 *en̄* G., but the stroke is gone.

9 *do[u . . . .]ka* G. In BanG II 2.7.1, Hintze suggests *do[udde]ka* or *do[uddel]ka*, infinitives of Future II. A trace of a letter can be discerned before *ka*: the extreme lower tip of a vertical or oblique slanting slightly to the left, it is compatible with *l*, and I therefore follow Hintze's suggestion and restore *do[udde]l̤ka*. For the construction cf. §152.b and see NI 78/35 ii 9 *enelka*.

gokou G., a misprint (correct in the Index, 124).

11 *on[esin ⟍] G.*, but a trace compatible with *i* remains after *on*, and before the break at the end of the line there is the upper part of a vertical. Tentatively I suggest *oni[snās]i̤[n]* (i.e. *onisnā* + *-sin*), as a translation of ὅτι ἠγάπησας; cf. 104.1-2n. (for *-sin* corresponding to ὅτι) and 106.8 and 115.12 (for *-sin* attached to an indicative).

12-13 *kosm[osl̄lon ek̄ka i]/ārimenalô* G. The lacuna, however, is too short for all this; we also expect *eiar-*, which G. avoided presumably because of limitations of space (see above, on 4-5). *kosm[osl̄lon* (or *kosm[osillon) ek̄] ārimenalô* suits the size of the lacuna. *ar-*, literally "grasp," here means "know"; cf. Dongolawi *ar*, where the same semantic range is observable (Armbruster, *Lex*. 17). See also lines 4 and 13 of the present page for the same verb.

13 *aïon ek̄[ka . . . . einn̄]-* G., but the lacuna cannot hold so many letters; it is suited to *ek̄ [ārise ⟍ einn]-*.

13-14 *einn̄]goul ke[talleeion] eia[* G. Here *eiar-*, not *ar-*, renders the Greek (ἔγνωσαν). As I have restored it, the line is somewhat short (though no shorter than lines 9 and 10); possibly the scribe added an intensive particle to the verb, e.g. *-lô* (§204.c), *-sn̄* (§277), or *-sô* (§279.a).

15 *ein*[G.; a likely restoration is [*aĭk eitreska* (107.12; cf. also above, line 5 and n.).

Below line 15, G. gives no indication of how many lines he assumed missing. An exempli-gratia reconstruction suggests that four lines are lost:

15   *ein* [*aĭk eitreska* ⟍ *pilligrātiğ*]   26
      [*ğise tekka ein tańska* ⟍ *on pilli*]
      [*grātiğğarre* ⟍ *onğou ein aĭk one*]
      [*sinⁱ teriā eñkonnoā* ⟍ *aïon teriā* ::]

      [*choiākn̄* : *k̄ê* : *āpos* : $\pm$ 13   ]   Heb 9:1

" . . . that you sent me. (26) I have revealed your name to them, and I will reveal it to them, in order that the love in which you loved me may be in them, and I in them. Choiak 28, Apostle . . . " (ὅτι σύ με ἀπέστειλας · (26) καὶ[1] ἐγνώρισα αὐτοῖς τὸ ὄνομά σου καὶ γνωρίσω, ἵνα ἡ ἀγάπη ἣν ἠγάπησάς με ἐν αὐτοῖς ᾖ κἀγὼ ἐν αὐτοῖς). Cf. 107.3-4, 11 (for *on*), St. 6.8-9 *p̄līgrātğ̆ğarra*, NI 78/26 i 17 (Jude 12) *oun onğilo* (= ἐν ταῖς ἀγάπαις ὑμῶν), L. 110.9-10 (for a construction similar to *onğou ein aĭk onesinⁱ*). I assume that a new lesson began in the last line; after *āpos* it would have held a translation of . . . μὲν οὖν [καὶ] ἡ πρώτη, for the continuation of which see the next page.

111

1 . . .]*ẹna* G., but the space can hold more, and the doubtful *e* may be *s*. [*konği*]*ṣṇā* suits the size of the lacuna and provides a translation of the Greek εἶχε; a faint trace remains of the stroke over *a*. For the text, which continues from the last line of the preceding page, see 110.15n.

---

[1] The conjunction καί is not always translated in Old Nubian (see 114.5-6n.), and it is here omitted in some witnesses (see Horner ad loc.).

2 .... *ā-* G., but the letters before *ā* are completely gone. [*sk̅ n*]*ā-* seems a likely restoration; it renders κοσμικόν interpreted as meaning "of the earth." *-na* instead of *-n* is surprising, but not without parallels: see BanG II 3.

3 *-ra*[.....]*lappa* G., but *ra* is not in the manuscript; it is restored presumably on the basis of line 8, but there *ṅaueira* is predicative. In the present passage the noun is apparently appositive to the subjective *-l* at the end of the lacuna, and so I have restored *ṅa*[*uei*]/[*rou* (for the usage see §65.b).

akdaktakarị[. G. Of the letter before the lacuna, the lower half of a vertical remains, extending slightly below the line. *i* is not at all likely; the traces resemble much more an *a*, and I suggest *akdaktakarạ*[*sṅ* ⟍, the perfect predicative participle. For the construction cf. K. 30.10-13 *einṅgoulappa ... kolatrasṅ* and 31.13-14 *einabba tĪlŌrô ettakrasin* (see §243).

[-]

4 .. *l*]*a* G. I propose [*tari*]*a*, i.e. *tar-la*; cf. below, 12-13n., and for the assimilation see §9.r.2. For the clause as a whole (*tariā ... douēsan*) cf. BanG II 2.4 n. 21, where Hintze feels that the *-na* after *-deken-* is "unerklärlich"; *-na* appears to mark the preceding as subject of the subjunctive *douēsan* (cf. BanG II 2.7.2), and *-dekel-* is often construed with noun endings (see my remarks in NON II 252 f.).

5 *-goul*: that this is added above the line was not reported by G.

6 *ṅ̄ssa*: here and in line 9 the singular suggests that the translator took the Greek as Ἁγία, not as Ἅγια (cf. the Bohairic version *tê etoumouti eros je t̲ê etouab*: see Horner^Boh).

7 *ouou-*: apparently the cardinal: see my note on NI 78/26 ii 7-8 in *STB* 2 (1980) 29.

9 *k*[*ouni*]*l* G., but a trace remains of the third letter; it is not compatible with *u* but suggests the lower right of *n*. I suggest *k*[*o*]*ṇ*[*ǧi*]*l*; for the plural infix cf. St. 28.10-29.1 *elǧaderou ṅaelde tītĪdekelka*, and especially gr. 4.1 *koṅǧra*.

10 *ṅạ*[*p* .]*ṛ* G.; the doubtfully read *r* can also be *o* (cf. especially the first *o* in *ouou-* in line 7); it is preceded by a faint, unidentifiable

speck. I propose *ṅa*[*p*]*ḳọ*, built upon the adjectival formation in -*ko* (see §59).

on G. There is a short stroke midway between *o* and *n*; presumably it should have been centered over *o*, as in 105.7.

[-]
igịrtn G.

11 [. . . . . . .]*tapa* G.; but traces of two letters precede. Of the first, an upper horizontal survives, suggesting *g*, *t* or *ṅ*. The second is probably *u*, less likely *ñ*, and there is room for an intervening *o*; we probably have a noun in the appositive corresponding to τὴν κιβωτόν (for the construction cf. 110.9-10).

12 [*p* . . . . . .] G. A possible restoration and interpretation is *na*/[*pika taddô*] *pigissan-* (i.e. *pi-gir-san*), "they caused gold to be upon it"; cf. BanG III 5.3.1 and K. 19.10 *trap͞ss͞idô p͞i-*.

12-13 *tari*[. . . . . .] G.; *tari*[*a* is suggested by Zyhlarz in §211; see also above, line 4. In both places *tariā* corresponds to ἐν ᾗ. It was probably followed here by *ṅapko*: see above, on line 10; if so, then
[-]
eme translates στάμνος. This word is not known to me elsewhere; its initial letter is much more likely to be *e* than *s*.

13 *mannan*: the third *n* is corrected or remade.

13-14 *da*/[. . . . .]*dou* G. Before *dou* there is an oblique stroke which suggests *a*, *d* or *l*. In §211 Zyhlarz cited this passage as follows: "Die Lokalisierung 'im Innern' erfolgt . . . an der Stelle: "*tar-i*[*a*] . . . . *au-ā da-l* 'in ihm . . . . darin befindlich' durch Umschreibung mit einem Wörtchen *au* unbekannter Bedeutung. Sinn etwa: 'in ihm . . . . als Inhalt befindlich' o. ä.'' Zyhlarz may be on the right track, but with *da*/[*l*, the word division is odd; and perhaps the scribe wrote *da*/*in*, a present subjunctive of which the subject is *mannan* (i.e. *mannan*<*a*?>: see above, on line 4): "manna being within."

15 G. does not record this line, of which only part of the last letter (apparently either *a* or *l*) survives. G. also does not mention how many lines he suspects are missing at the bottom of the page. I calculate that below line 15 probably three lines are lost; even an exempli-gratia

reconstruction for much of this section is hardly realistic. But the text may have been arranged as follows: lines 14 and 15 probably contained a translation of καὶ ἡ ῥάβδος 'Ααρὼν ἡ βλαστήσασα καὶ αἱ πλάκες τῆς διαθήκης, 16 and 17 could have rendered ὑπεράνω δὲ αὐτῆς Χερουβὶν δόξης κατασκιάζοντα τὸ ἱλαστήριον, and the last line, 18, may have been [-*goul dekenna douēsan* \\ *ten* (or *einn*)], continued by *ǧourika* on 112.1. For the general structure see above, lines 4-6. Admittedly, this is purely hypothetical; it is possible that *dou* at the end of line 14 is the subjunctive of the relative clause, and if it is, then the entire recon-struction is subject to modification.

112

[-]
Page number: : *rib* : G.
1 For a possible restoration of the text before *ǧourika* see 111.15n.
2 G. simplifies the ornamental series closing the line and prints:
— . . . —

3-5 This section is abbreviated from the first lesson in the Lection-ary as now preserved. Note that for τοῦ δὲ 'Ιησοῦ Χριστοῦ [the Nubian has simply [*t*]$\overline{lln}$ "of God."

5 G. inadvertently omits *choiākn̄* : : $\overline{kd}$: : *par*^{t} : : —, though he lists *par*^{t} in his Index, 114. The phrase is printed as *choiākn̄* : $k\bar{d}$: *par*^{t} :

by Schäfer-Schmidt, *Handschriften* 604; they note that *par*^{t} "ist eine Abkürzung für das nubische *partakesin* 'es ist geschrieben'." Their resolution is presumably modelled on 104.5 *partakesin kellô*. But the present passage requires the indicative, and probably we should resolve as *partakisnā* (K. 22.14) or *partakona* (NI 74/14.2.1: Plumley, *New Light* Plate LV).

6 ff. G. numbers this and the following lines on the page one digit too high, and he also omits the ornamental stroke pattern separat-ing this section from the preceding; in an earlier transcript he doubt-less included the stroke pattern, numbering it as line 6: see 115.4n.

6 *apoŝ* G. (with *t* written above)

8 In the clause divider after *ounnoutaka* the red stroke precedes the black, contrary to the usual pattern (see above, p. 19).

8-9 *te[ē?]dn̄* G. The sheet breaks off after *te*, and the space available can accommodate a second *e*. Since the scribe wrote *teēd-* in 103.4 he could have done so here as well. But in line 9 he has *ted-*, and this is also the spelling elsewhere in the extant corpus: 103.6; K. 26.13-14; Plumley, *Nubian Literary Text* B 10 (Rev 14:12); possibly fr. 2 b 7 (in St. 15.2 *tedka = tekka*).

9 *tauô̄²*: *tauô* G. (also in Index, 118).

10 *tlln̄* G. (*tll̄n̄* in Index, 119).

totkanek: to the right of the final *k* there is a small blot of ink; it is probably not intentional. (It is not reported by G.)

10-11 *etkoannoā*: 3rd pers. pl.; for the divergence from the Greek, which here has ἀπολάβωμεν, see §184 Anm.

11-12 [. .]*nosin* G.; for the restoration see §§161.a and 278.

12 G. prints *e[n]* but gives the Greek as ὑμῶν. The latter requires *oun*: cf. 101.11 (and see note ad loc.). For the variant ἡμῶν the Nubian should be *en* (St. 1.3, 2.12; cf. 108.5), not *ēn*, which is the 2nd pers. sg. Careful examination of the exiguous traces leads me to print *e[n]* as being slightly preferable as a reading to *o[un]*, but I must emphasize that *o[un]* cannot be excluded.

13 *eiṭ[r̄sn]a* G. The stroke and part of the *s* survive.

13-14 *eint[. . .]krou ạ[. . . . .]* G., but there is no space in the manuscript after *krou*; *a* is paleographically possible, but with it we should expect a supraliteral stroke (see NON VIII 56), and so I have preferred to read *kroul*, a participle. Perhaps we should articulate and restore as follows: *ein t[ara] kr-oul*, "this which comes forth and shouts" (i.e. an expansion of κράζον); cf. St. 29.12-30.1 *kr̄seu-ēt-* and Plumley, *Nubian Literary Text* A 16 *ouā* (= *ououā* in M. 11.5 *kiā ououā*).

15 *en̄[* G. After *n̄* I discern the upper tip of a vertical.

Below line 15, G. notes: "[Several lines lost.]" I tentatively assume that *eint*[+ 3]*krouḷ* contains a translation of κρᾱζον. Thereafter reconstruction is hazardous, but I venture to suggest the following:

	krouḷ [*ab*]*ḫạ pạ*[*po* ∖ *endô ošoṅatta*]	7
15	*eṅṃ*[*enna* ∖ *tota eṅnaenkô* ∖ *tota*]	
	[*eṅennon tḷlilôğôā seuattaketal*]	
	[*eṅna* + ornamental series (as in 112.2)]	

$$[\textit{choiākn} : \overline{ki}^{\,t} : \textit{mat} : \overline{d} : \overline{i}\textit{esousieion}] \qquad \text{Mt 2:1}$$

" . . . crying: 'Abba, Father.' (7) For this reason you are not a slave, but you are a son, and if you are a son, you are also an heir through God. Choiak 29, Matthew 4: And Jesus . . . " (. . . κρᾱζον · ἀββὰ ὁ πατήρ. (7) ὥστε οὐκέτι εἶ δοῦλος ἀλλὰ υἱός · εἰ δὲ υἱός, καὶ κληρονόμος διὰ θεοῦ. [Mt 2:1] τοῦ δὲ 'Ιησοῦ . . .). Cf. M. 12.12 (*eṅdô* = "dessentwegen"—Zyhlarz, Text I S. 50); St. 20.9-10 (*ōšoṅaeigoun* = δούλων — Zyhlarz, Text III S. 42 n. 1; cf. §§41, 45); 105.2-3 (*tḷlilôğôā*). For the lack of assimilation in *eṅṃ*[*enna* cf. Plumley, *Nubian Literary Text* B 5 *einmssana-* (this should be read in place of the editor's *eilimssana-*). The Greek text offers several variants to διὰ θεοῦ: διὰ θεὸν, διὰ ('Ιησοῦ) Χριστοῦ, θεοῦ διὰ ('Ιησοῦ) Χριστοῦ, μὲν θεοῦ συγκληρονόμος δὲ Χριστοῦ; see NA^*app* for details. Any of these alternatives, if it formed the basis of the Old Nubian, could be accommodated within the number of lines assumed in the above reconstruction. A longer phrase would simply result in a decrease in the length of the ornamental series in line 17. For the Ammonian number in line 18 see Schäfer-Schmidt, *Handschriften* 605.

113

Page number: : *riḡ* : G.
1 For the beginning of this section see 112.15n.
ioudaiạ[*n*]- G.
2 *oukrigoulô* G. (also in Index, 112).
2-3 [. .]*sn̄* G., who has [*ei?*]*sn̄* in his Index (97); Zyhlarz prints

the passage in §284 with *eisn̄*. For *eissn̄* see above, 100.1n. The line can easily hold *eis* at the end.

3 *tara* is certain, and *tarl̄* cannot be read.

4 *iērousalmiō . . . pesrāgou[e]* G.; the final *e* may have been elided, as in 101.3.

5-6 *ourouou ounnoutakol*: "the king who has been born"; for the construction cf. K. 29.11 *tl̄lou takka auol-*.

10 *[i]ērousalmê* G. Of the diaeresis over *i* the right dot remains.

[-]
12 *kptn̄* G.

13 [. . .]*ligara* G. What he took as *l* survives only in the upper part, and the remnants are also compatible with *m*. A supraliteral stroke precedes. I propose *[tm̄]migara* "causing to assemble" as a translation of συναγαγών. This causative formation appears elsewhere in WN 21 (see BanG III 5.3.1) and in NI 78/5 b ii 2 *tm̄migaǧǧa* (= -*gar-ǧ-a*).

[*tek*]*ka* G.

ēgidǧisnā: what I take as a stroke over *e* is faded and may possibly not be ink.

14 Schäfer-Schmidt, *Bruchstücke* 782, read *ounnou]takonoā*, an anomalous formation. On purely paleographical grounds, the remnant of the penultimate letter is compatible with *a*, *o* and probably *l*. For the conjunction with the interrogative particle -*ā* see §§173 and 175.

Note that for the clause marker the scribe has reversed the normal sequence and has placed red before black (see above, p. 19).

15 . . . . *ioudai* G. There are, however, more letters in the lacuna than G. indicated; my restoration is modelled on M. 14.15-16 *tadgl̄ pesesn̄-*; also possible is *takka pessana*: see Sunnarti 2.6 (as revised by me in ZPE 37 [1980] 173-178). Schäfer-Schmidt, *Bruch-*

??
stücke 782, restored [*targille pessana . bêthlēmê*] *ioudai/[nno* (where . represents the clause marker), but *targille* is too long for the lacuna.

16 For this line G. prints merely . . ., but an *a* is clearly visible as the last letter of the line; it was read by Schäfer-Schmidt, *Bruchstücke* 782. The restoration which I put in the text fits the size of the lacuna;

instead of *partakisnāsn̄*, the scribe may have written *partakonasn̄*: see on 112.5 and for -*sn̄* see 106.8n.

Below line 16, originally there were probably three lines. After [*kisnāsn̄* (?), the remainder of 17 could hold a translation of διὰ τοῦ προφήτου · καὶ σὺ (e.g. — *p̄rophêtêslokô* \ *eikketal*]), and a rendering of Βηθλέεμ, γῆ ᾽Ιούδα, οὐδαμῶς could fit in 18 (e.g. [*bêthlēmê ioudana s̄kīa* + equivalent of οὐδαμῶς]; cf. BanG II 2.6.1 for -*na* . . . -*a*). For the remaining text, ἐλαχίστη εἶ ἐν τοῖς ἡγεμόσιν ᾽Ιούδα · ἐκ σοῦ γὰρ ἐξελεύσεται ἡγούμενος, probably two lines would have sufficed, of which the second would belong to the beginning of the next page (e.g. [*mekkil dounna ioudan* + word for ἡγεμών]/[*goullo* \ *eiriāketal km̄masn̄* + word for ἡγούμενος]; cf. 103.6, 104.5-6, 106.8n., 110.1).

114

Line number: [: *rid* :] G.

1 For a tentative reconstruction of this line see 113.16n.

2 *io*]*uddil̬* G., but the space at the beginning of the line is suitable for only one letter. Read [*e*]*uddil*: cf. NI 78/26 i 18 (Jude 12), where *eur*[*il* renders ποιμαίνοντες; for the verb see BanG III 6.1.1.

After *io*]*uddil̬* G. read *a*[. . . . . *ēr*/*ôd*]*ê*. The lacuna should hold more letters, and G.'s word division between the lines is odd, especially since we have room for only one letter at the beginning of the third line. I have restored exempli gratia; cf. gr. 9.3 *tan totou n̊al* and see §65.a.

3 *dogdr*[G.; *dogdr*[*ikouka* appears in the Index, 93. Of the diaeresis over *i* (cf. 113.3), the left dot remains.

4 . .]*un*[. . G., with no attempt to indicate the amount of text lost after [; this practice is in evidence elsewhere on this page and the next.

4-5 . . /*t*]*auoukka*[. . G.

5-6 . .]/*eitari*[. . G. For this section my restoration is exempli gratia; cf. 109.6-7 *kosmo*[*s*]*lāgil aïk eitrēsin*-, and note that καί at the beginning of verse 8 need not be translated in Old Nubian: cf. 106.9-10. For *ǧora* cf. e.g. M. 12.14.

6-7 *totn̄ ǧou*]*rika*: so G. in his Index (114, s.v. *paǧ*-, *paǧǧ*-); in his text he has only . .]*ǧou*/*rika*, with the bracket misplaced.

7 *paǧǧann̦[asô*: I follow G.'s restoration given in his Index, 114; his text has merely *paǧǧann̦[* . . For the formation cf. §172 concerning *oulgn̄nasô* for **oulg-r-ana-sô* and also St. 29.10 *tannasô* for **tar-ana-sô*. Here we have the verb *paǧ-gar-*, comparable to *paǧei-paǧi-gr̄-* in K. 33.3-4 (see BanG III 5.3.1).

After *paǧǧann̦[asô* perhaps the scribe added a postpositional phrase modifying the imperative and corresponding to ἀκριβῶς.

8-9 *ṅprti̦[* . . . . *]/sộ* G. (the verb is spelled correctly in the Index, 90). Before the lacuna *a* is a possible reading; with it we have the normal form of the adjunctive (cf. K. 29.14). The lacuna is much longer than G. indicated; my hypothetical restoration corresponds to the Greek ἀπαγγείλατέ μοι (instead of *aïgil*, *aïka* is also possible: see 113.15n.).

9-10 *[a]ïketal ki̦[* . . . . G., without indication of how much text is lost, and then . . *]/e[* . . . . After *e* in line 10 I discern what can be the left part of *t*, and I have tentatively restored *eț[koïōā*, "in order that I may bring"; the end of the preceding line will then have contained a direct and an indirect object (e.g. "honor *aut sim.* to him"). I cannot reconcile the writing with a form of *douk-*, used in 113.8 to render προσκυνεῖν. If *eț[koïōā* is right, the translator has resorted to paraphrase. After *eț[koïōā* I have attempted a hypothetical reconstruction of the text corresponding to the beginning of verse 9; cf. 113.9.

11 *ǧôriș[ana* G. in Index, 126; *ǧôriș[* . . appears in the text. The *s* seems inevitable; it is followed by a trace not incompatible with *a*.

11-13 . . *]/oskl̦[o* . . . . .] *n[* . . . *]eriōr̦[* . . *]/āri[* . . .] ⟍ G. My exempli-gratia restoration suits the size of the lacuna. The space seems too narrow for *eissn̄* (see 100.1n.); for *eis* + *-lon* (12) cf. especially Plumley, *Nubian Literary Text* A 14-15 *ēs aggelosn̄ touskītīllon*. For *mašal]oskl̦[ō* see 113.3. The phrase *oueiñǧil . . . ṅl̦]ș[a]n̦-* (in which the final *n* is fairly certain) corresponds to ὁ ἀστὴρ ὃν εἶδον and is structurally comparable to St. 16.4-5 *kark au̦[l]endrā einn̄*; see also 108.9n. For *ṅl̄-* instead of *ṅal-* (for which the space is not adequate) cf. M. 10.15 *ṅlsna*. After *t]eriō* "in their midst," the stroke could be the left side of *k*, and so, exempli gratia, I propose *k̦[iā*; cf. K. 25.13 as well as line 9 above.

[-]

As regards *ārisṇa*, autoptic examination revealed that the final *a* is all but inevitable; it is preceded by three badly damaged letters which at least could be *isn*. For the absence of the plural infix -*ğ*- cf. 109.8 *eitasse*.

13 *totn̄ ḳengoul k*[. . . .] G. Note the plural, as in 110.8 *dou*[*te*]-*goullô*.

14 *okimeğ̆ğa* G.

[*pauouka*]: so G. (cf. 100.12, 103.5, 112.5). Unless the writing is cramped or *pauka* (cf. M. 7.15) was written, there is probably no room for the clause divider at the end of this line.

15 After *ṅalen* G. prints [. . . . .]; before the lacuna there is a trace of an additional letter, not incompatible with the upper left of *n*, and so I tentatively restore -*ṇ*[*on piskane*] (cf. above, line 8 *ēlennon*, and 108.13, where *piskane* renders χαρά, as in the present passage.

16 *dau*[. . . . . G. For *dauēl*- see BanG IV 5.2 and cf. e.g. K. 28.14-15 *arm̄skire dauēl-lo*; for -*lo* see also K. 25.6-8 *ounna mig̃rkeilo pağanaso*.

Below line 16 estimation of the material presumed missing (all of verse 11) suggests that it would fit on five lines, of which the last belongs on the top of the following page. G. gives no indication of how much text he judged was lost.

115

1 . .] . . . . [. . G., but no trace remains of the line.

2 . .]ọouann[. . G.; here and elsewhere on this page, G. does not always attempt to show how much text is lost (see also my note to 114.4). Perhaps we have]ọouann[*on*], corresponding to καὶ χρηματι-σθέντες; cf. §158.2.

3 . .]eā ⟍ s̄d[. . G. Here the clause divider has the red stroke before the black, contrary to usual practice (see above, p. 19). For the context see Stricker 448.

4 . .] . *ese* . [. . G. Of the first letter, the lower part of a vertical survives, and the last suggests *t* or perhaps *g*; if the latter, then pos-

sibly we have] . *eseg*[*l̄*, i.e. the ending of a phrase corresponding to εἰς τὴν χώραν αὐτῶν.

G. marks as line 5 what is in fact the decorative stroke which appears elsewhere between sections. His text reads: [—..]— The remaining lines of his edition of this page are therefore one number too high.

5 [*choiakn̄* ..]*ntotka* G. In his text G. prints all of verse 3 of the Greek, with parentheses around διὰ τῆς σαρκός; to the latter he attaches a note: "These three words omitted by some." But the manuscript scarcely has room for all of this, and if the heading follows the usual pattern, the lesson began with *ta*]*n totka*; i.e. the Old Nubian translated only τὸν ἑαυτοῦ υἱὸν πέμψας κτλ. and omitted the first part of the verse (τὸ γὰρ ἀδύνατον τοῦ νόμου ἐν ᾧ ἠσθένει διὰ τῆς σαρκός, ὁ θεός).

6 [........ *l*]*a outoureitra* G. I have restored exempli gratia; for *kolat*- "likeness" cf. Plumley, *Nubian Literary Text* B 21 (Rev 14:14) *eitn̄ totn̄ kolat*- (ὅμοιον υἱῷ ἀνθρώπου).

7 [........ *n̄*]*apeka* G.; in his Greek text he brackets καὶ περὶ ἁμαρτίας and adds the note: "These three words omitted by some." G. has underestimated the size of the lacuna; as I have hypothetically restored it, it can hold a translation of περὶ ἁμαρτίας (for the omission of καὶ see the apparatus to the Greek) ... ἐν τῇ σαρκί: *napeldô gadlō* (for -*ldô* see BanG IV 5.3.3 and for *gad-lō* cf. St. 27.9).

7-8 *middon*/[........ *tedn̄*] G. If the Nubian reflects the Greek accurately, *middon*[+ 3 stands for κατέκρινεν. Perhaps the scribe wrote *middon*/*na*, i.e. *middol-na*, but I have no precise parallel to this construction, which is analogous to the future formation consisting of the future participle + present endings (see BanG V 2.2.b). Before *tedn̄* I have restored *eriā*, to correspond to ἐν ἡμῖν; cf. e.g. 110.3.

9-10 *konnoā* (sic, without brackets) ..*kega*]*grā ğ*[....]*rmi*/ [.... [*seuartn̄ kegagrā le*]*ṇkô* \ G. I can discern a trace of the letter before *rmi*: a vertical stroke, slanting slightly upward to the left, it suggests *a* or *o*. Possibly the scribe wrote *ğokar*-, a compound of *ğo*- and *kar*- (see §300 for the formation and cf. *ğoğoki* in M. 16.10, which may mean "coming and going," i.e. "continually"). However we restore it, the word is likely to be continued as -*mi*[*nil*; the complex renders τοῖς μὴ ... περιπατοῦσιν (for the singular cf. §329). Instead of *enkô* the scribe may have written *lenkô*; with the latter there may not have been room for the clause divider (see on 107.15-16).

11 [. . . . .]*oulgo*[. . . . *gadn̄ n̄*]*eeigou-* G. Before *-oul* there is a low horizontal which is most likely to be associated with *d* (cf. *-do-* in line 7 above). The verb *dou-* "be" is therefore probably involved, and I tentatively suggest [*gad* . (.)] (perhaps [*gadn̄*]) *doulgo*[*us*]*sin̤* (i.e. *-goul-sin*: cf. on 108.7), "for those who are (of?) the flesh . . . " For *-sin̤* followed by *-sin* (next line) see §278. I have no precise parallel for *gadn̄ dou-*, though it may have some support from the nisbe formation in 12, *se*]*uartn̄*; the scribe may have written *gadlā* "in the flesh."

12 *-k*[.]*nnasin̤* G., for which Zyhlarz suggests *-k*[*i*]*nnasin̤* (cf. §277), a compound of *kir-* (see Glossar, 178; cf. also BanG III 5.2); he may be right, but the absence of a parallel makes certainty impossible. The verb is singular because the subject is a generic plural; for the usage see my remarks in NON IV 39.[1] The particle *-sin* renders γάρ; cf. 106.8n.

12-13 *se*]*uartn̄* [. . . . . . *s*]*euartn̄ka* G. For the nisbe formation cf. e.g. K. 23.10 *iereōsinka* and gr. 9.1 *tan̄ṣou papn̄no on n̄annilo* "in the name of the Father and in that of the Son."

13-14 *kourki*[. . . . . . .]*n* G. *kourki-* suggests *kourki*/[*on*, as at the end of line 14 (see next note); if rightly restored, *-*[*on* may reflect δέ in the Greek, not the usual γάρ (see the apparatus). For *diar-* "death" see 105.12 and cf. K. 24.6; for *-sin* functioning as a copula cf. K. 30.7-8 *ākossa-sn̄* and 30.9 *oukkatta-sin̄*.

14 *kourkion*: i.e. *kourkī-on*; cf. §11 and also *eigeirion* in K. 29.14.

15 [. . . . . *ga*]*dn̄* G.; two supraliteral strokes can be discerned above the lacuna.

16 At the end of this line there is a faint trace of a letter, possibly *n*; it was not noted by G.

---

[1] Note that the reading which I there propose for the present passage, [*gadn̄g*]*oullō* [*ap̤*]*p̤a*, cannot be justified paleographically.

INDEX OF NEW WORDS

PLATES

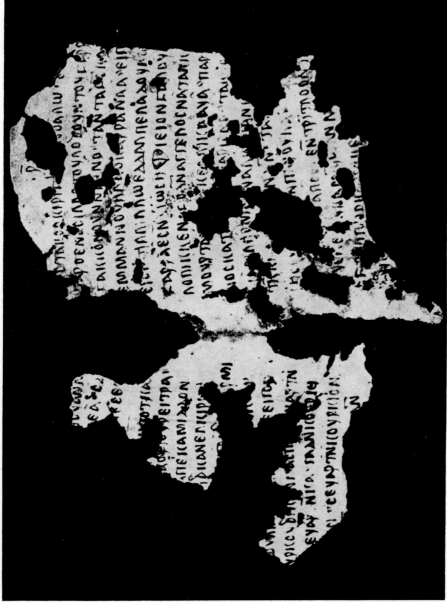

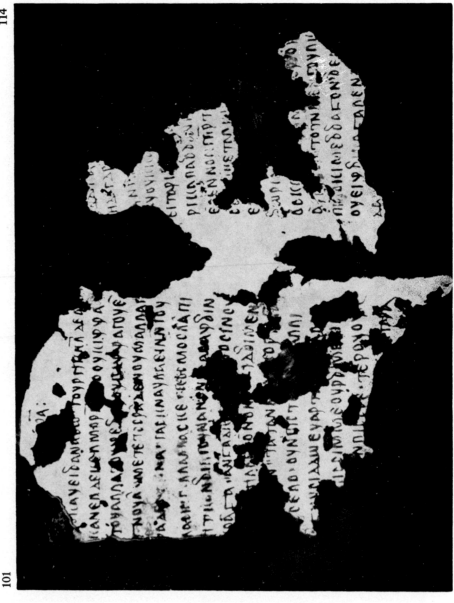

113 102

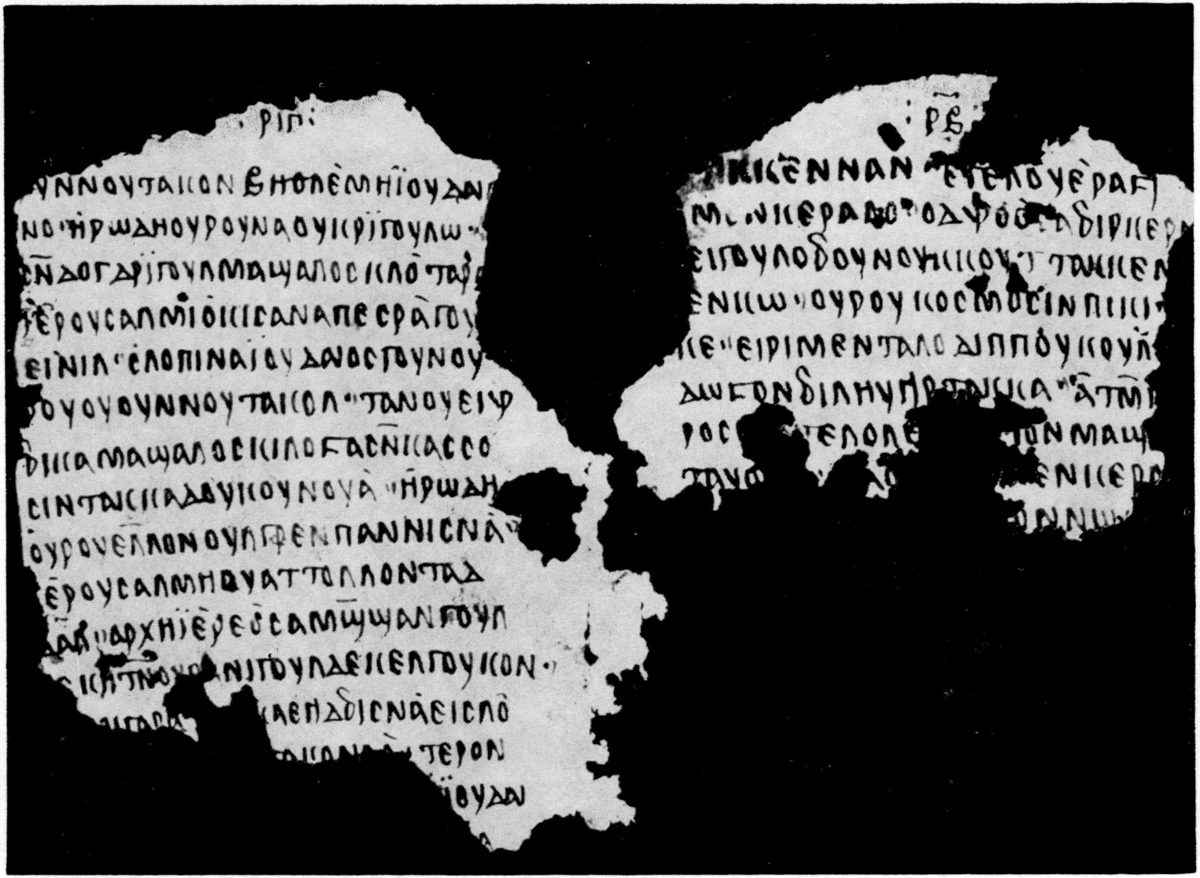

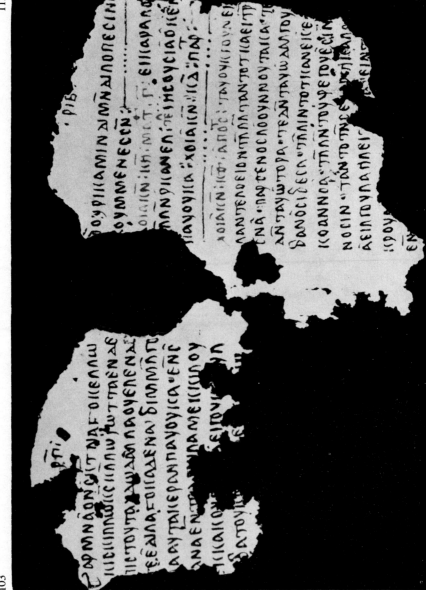

V

111 104

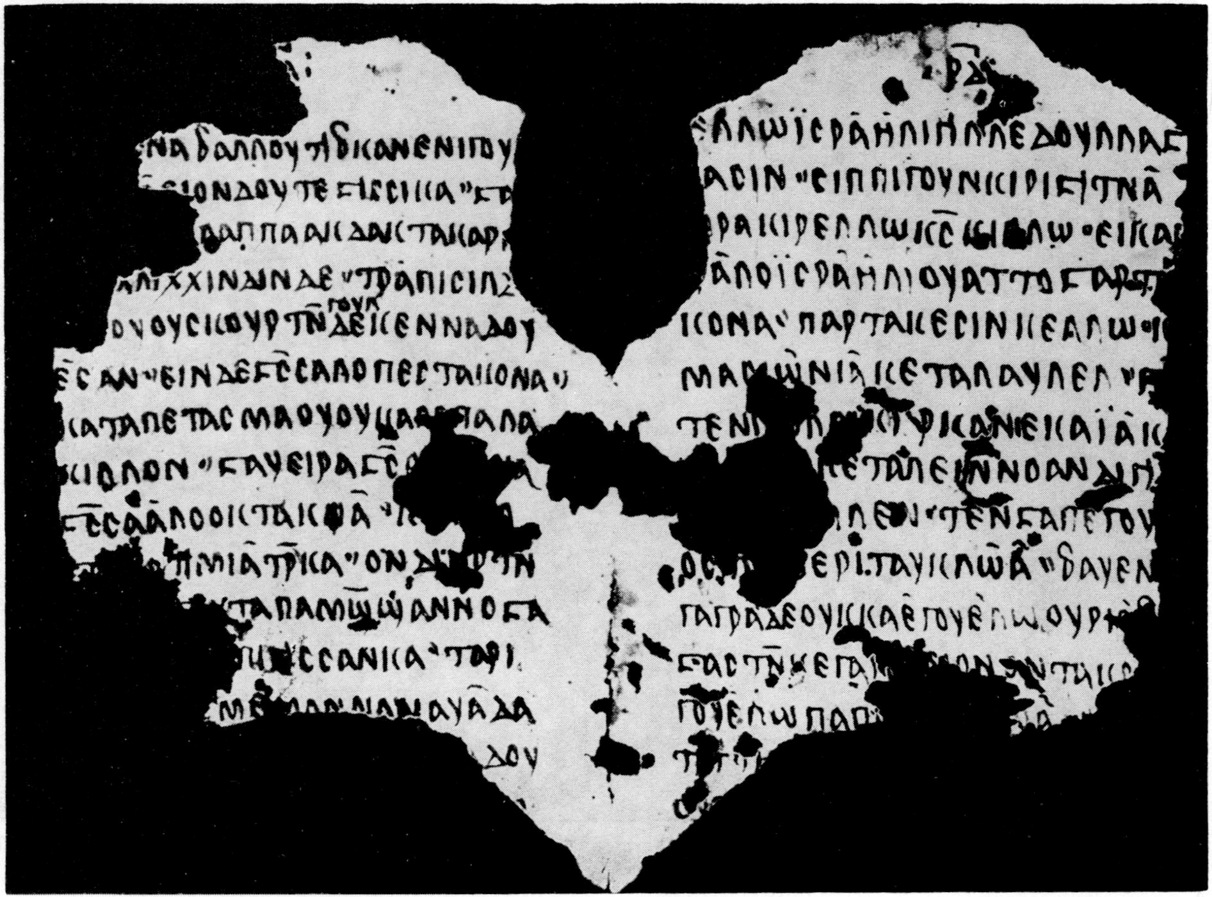

105 110

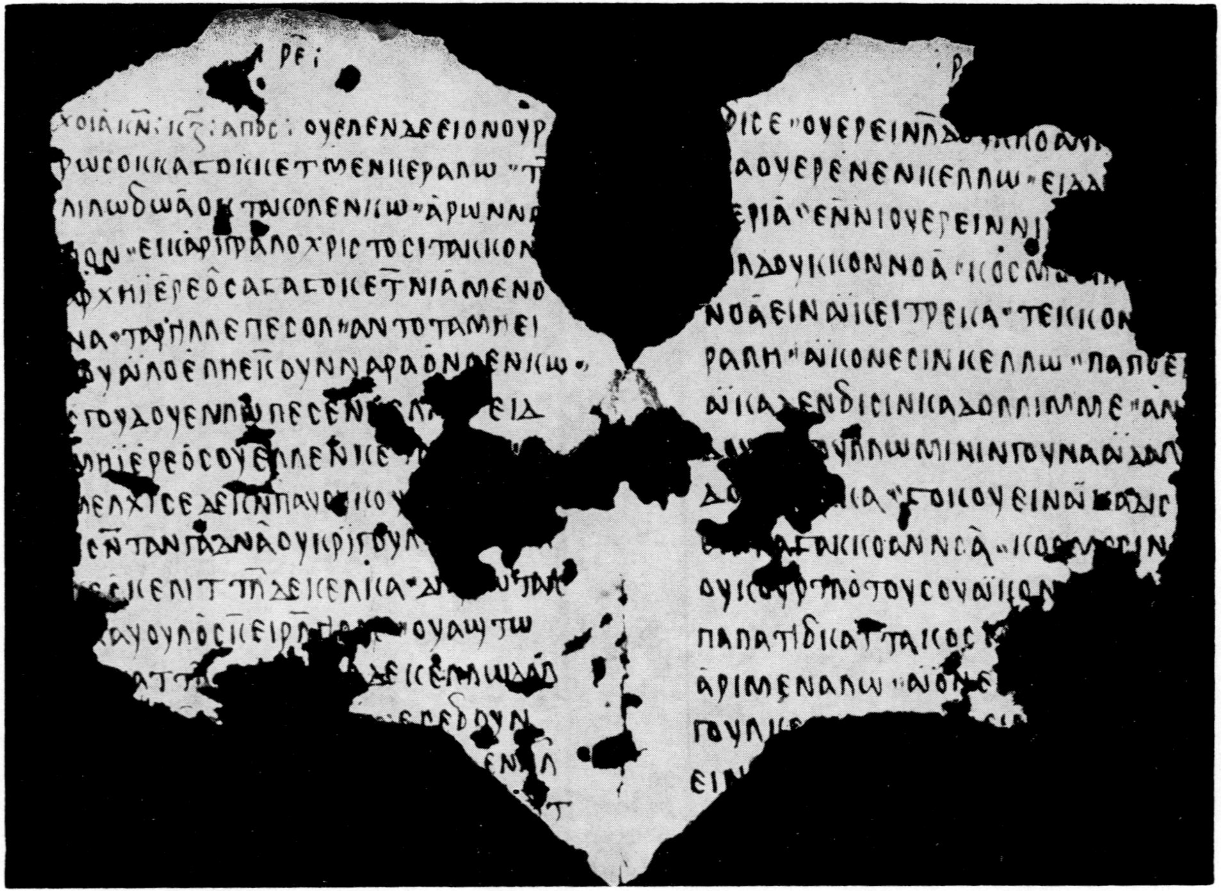

109 106

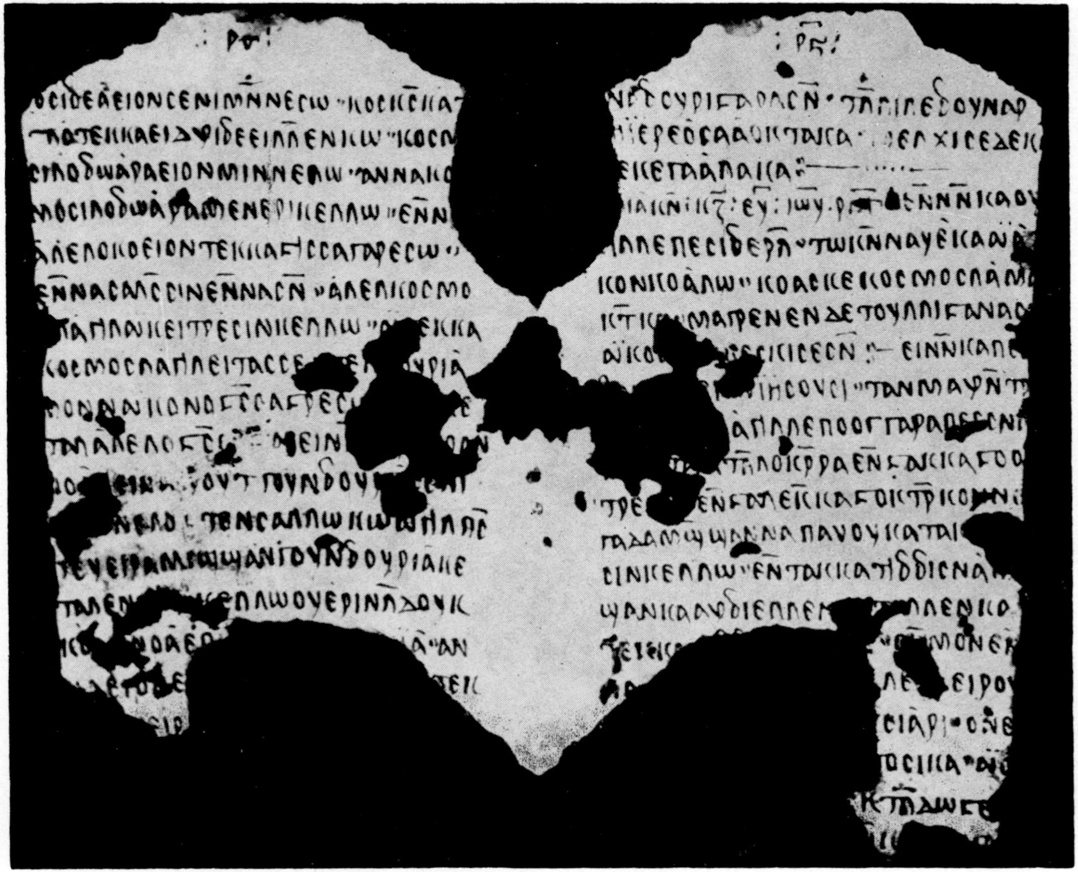

107 108

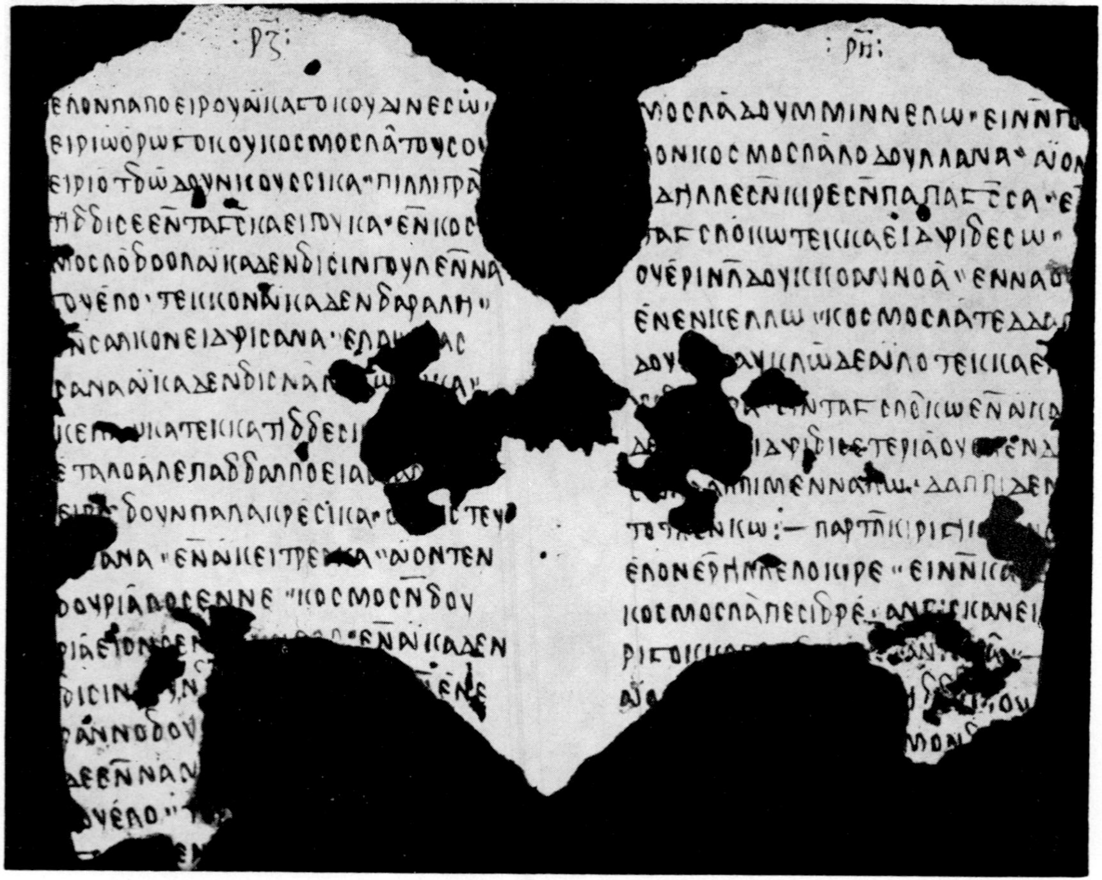